SHELLEY BOETTCHER

UNCORKED!

**The Definitive Guide to Alberta's
Best Wines under $25**

whitecap

Editing by Sarah Maitland
Cover and interior design by Setareh Ashrafologhalai
Typesetting by Jesse Marchand

Many of the wine label images were provided by wineries and distributors and are
reprinted with permission. Others were photographed by the author.

Printed in Canada at Friesens

Library and Archives Canada Cataloguing in Publication

Boettcher, Shelley, 1970–
    Uncorked! : the definitive guide to Alberta's best wines under $25
/ Shelley Boettcher.

Includes index.
ISBN 978-1-77050-031-0

    1. Wine and wine making. 2. Wine and wine making—Alberta.
I. Title.

TP548.B63 2010   641.2'2   C2010-904677-3

The publisher acknowledges the financial support of the Government of Canada
through the Canada Book Fund (CBF) and the Province of British Columbia through
the Book Publishing Tax Credit.

10 11 12 13 14   5 4 3 2 1

CONTENTS

INTRODUCTION

You're holding in your hands a guide to buying 150 wines that each cost $25 or less, plus suggestions for wine and food pairings, and more.

Buying wine doesn't have to be pretentious, boring, and expensive—unless you want it to be. Yes, I appreciate a first-growth Bordeaux just as much as the next wine geek (especially if it's on someone else's tab), but I don't like to be bored, and I'm always looking for a good deal. If you also love a deal, you'll appreciate this book. It's filled with my favourite bargain wines in the Alberta market.

Why so many red wines in the book? Because we Canucks drink more red wine than any other kind. And because I like red wine. So there.

Don't be disappointed if your favourite bargain wine isn't listed in this book; there are literally hundreds and hundreds of wines for $25 and under available in Alberta. It would take a mighty long list to include all the great wines sold in the province.

And keep in mind, vintages may change as stock sells out at certain stores, but don't worry if you find a different vintage of the same label. For the most part, the wineries featured here are consistent producers, year after year.

Although prices were verified at press time, they may not always be exact. (Alberta's liquor market is privatized, which means retailers don't have to charge the same price at every store. A $22 bottle at one store could be $27 at another. Shop around.)

Still, you get the picture; in these pages, you'll find excellent wines at steal-of-a-deal prices. So dig in. Buy a bottle, or a case or two. And enjoy.

Tear down the stack of pretentious wine reviews you've attached to your fridge door. Crumple them up. Put them in the recycling bin. You're far too sexy to be bored by the search for a good bottle.

—Shelley

HOW TO USE THIS BOOK

How should you read this book? You could read all the way through from start to finish, if you like. If you're a wine geek already, you can read up on whatever specific grape variety you're into at the moment by flipping to the index. You can browse by price or by country. You could choose a wine by the occasion, whether it be Grandma's birthday party, a first date, or your book club—I've listed a bunch for each wine under the "Uncork" heading. Or, if you want to check out some of my favourites, turn to page 162 for a list of my desert-island wines. Or you can just look at the pretty labels.

The main heading for each wine reflects the most prominent piece of information displayed on each wine's label. Sometimes it's the name of the winery and other times it is the name of the wine itself. That may seem inconsistent, but since labelling practices differ so widely, it's meant to help you find the bottle more easily in the store.

I've also made a note of the kind of closure that the wine uses, as a point of interest. These are depicted by the following icons:

 Traditional cork

 Screw-cap closure

 Champagne / Sparkling wine cork

 Flip-top trigger closure

10 TIPS ON CELLARING YOUR WINE

1. *Keep wine out of the kitchen (unless you're opening it).*
   Corkscrews? Yes. Wine? No. Your kitchen is too warm (and probably too busy). It's not the best place in which to store wine properly.

2. *Store your wine in the coolest part of your house.*
   Under the spare-bedroom bed or in a spare closet will work if you don't have a basement, or room for a wine fridge.

3. *Garages are for cars, not cuvées.*
   Unless your garage is heated, it's too cold in the winter. You'll freeze everything. And your wine can pick up icky smells like car exhaust or mice or just plain ol' dust. Your garage is for empties—until you ship 'em off to a grateful Boy Scout or cash 'em in for money to buy a few new vintages.

4. *Tip 'em over. Gently.*
   They're not bowling pins. Lay your bottles gently on their sides so their corks touch the wine at all times. (Not a big deal if you mostly have screw caps.)

5. *Turn off the lights.*
   Keep the room dark. Too much light will fade your pretty labels and oxidize the wines.

6. *Stay away from the cat box, the dog bed, mothballs, and oil paints.*
   Strong smells will seep into your wines. Cat pee may be a desirable odour in some Sauvignon Blanc wines (I'm serious), but let the winemaker decide that. Not you. Or your cat.

7. *Jiggle elsewhere.*
   Above your washing machine? Or beside your treadmill? Not good. The vibration can damage the corks.

4

8. *Get wet.*

Humidity keeps corks from drying out, and in the cold, dry climate of Alberta, that's important. If you can't afford a humidifier, put a bucket or two of water in your "cellar." The moisture will help maintain good humidity.

9. *Planning to buy a wine fridge? Consider size and noise.*

How many bottles do you plan to keep at one time? Does the unit have racks that will fit whatever it is that you prefer to drink? How loud is it when it runs?

10. *Money's no object? Then shop.*

Hire a professional. Myriad companies out there will build professional cellars with humidity and temperature controls. Shop around. Ask friends and restaurant staff. Google.

FIRST, THE RED WINES

BLUE MOUNTAIN

Blue Mountain Vineyard and Cellars
....
WINERY

Gamay Noir   2009
....
VARIETY   YEAR

Okanagan Valley, B.C. $25
....
ORIGIN   PRICE   CLOSURE

If you've ever had a Beaujolais wine from France, you've had wine made from Gamay Noir grapes. Here's an outstanding Canuck version—all spice and raspberries. A good wine for white wine fans because it's low in tannins, the stuff that makes your mouth feel dry when you drink red wine.

TRIVIA Blue Mountain is a 100 percent Canadian, 100 percent family-owned winery, owned by the Mavetys, who started off growing grapes for other people before setting up their own gig in 1991.

PAIR WITH Roast chicken, veal, ham, salmon.

UNCORK For Canada Day, book club, dinner with wine geeks. Or stick in the cellar for four to six years.

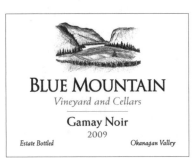

BLUE MOUNTAIN
Vineyard and Cellars
Gamay Noir
2009
Estate Bottled   Okanagan Valley

FORK IN THE ROAD

Fork in the Road	Oliver Block 249	
WINERY	WINE NAME	
red blend (see below)	2008	
VARIETY	YEAR	
Okanagan Valley, B.C.	$22	
ORIGIN	PRICE	CLOSURE

A side project from the folks at Mission Hill Family Estate's Artisan Wine Company, this is a plush, ripe, juicy easy-drinking red wine with zero pretensions and a screw-cap closure to boot. A berry-packed blend of Merlot, Syrah, Cabernet Franc, Cabernet Sauvignon, and Petit Verdot, it spent almost a year and a half in oak, which gives it nice soft tannins and yummy vanilla-coffee aromas.

TRIVIA There are more than fourteen different types of forks (including your everyday kitchen forks, plus those specifically designed for the likes of pickles, fondues, oysters, and salads), not including all the forks unrelated to food, such as pitchforks and tuning forks. Then there's yet another sort of fork—the fork in the road. Take the direction that leads to good wine.

PAIR WITH Stew, meaty casserole, cassoulet, or just sip by itself.

UNCORK For book clubs, Friday night dinners, barbecues, family get-togethers, last-minute dinners with friends, hump day (aka Wednesday).

GANTON AND LARSEN PROSPECT WINERY

Ganton and Larsen Prospect Winery	Fats Johnson	
WINERY	WINE NAME	
Pinot Noir	2008	
VARIETY	YEAR	
Okanagan Valley, B.C.	$19	
ORIGIN	PRICE	CLOSURE

You won't read about it on the label, but the gang at Mission Hill Family Estate Winery started Ganton and Larsen Prospect Winery as a side project, one of the wineries under their Artisan Wine Company moniker. (See Fork in the Road on the previous page for another one from this company.) The Prospect Winery wines are named for two families of grape growers that were instrumental during Mission Hill's early years.

As for the wine, it's light, very light, and smells like strawberries. Very soft tannins, very easy to sip.

TRIVIA According to the label, Fats Johnson was a kind older man who used to hand out doughnuts to the neighbourhood kids. Hmm . . . doughnuts. One can only speculate on how he earned the nickname "Fats."

PAIR WITH Roast chicken, roast vegetables, grilled salmon, seared tuna.

UNCORK Now, or for family gatherings, book clubs, hump day (aka Wednesday).

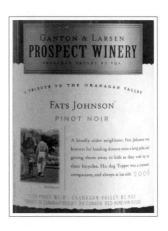

GRAY MONK

Gray Monk Estate Winery	Latitude 50	
WINERY	WINE NAME	
red blend	2008	
VARIETY	YEAR	
Okanagan Valley, B.C.	$19	
ORIGIN	PRICE	CLOSURE

The name of this winery comes from the Austrian and Hungarian translation for Pinot Gris, *Grauar Mönch*, which literally translates to "Gray Monk" in English. One of three Latitude 50 blends (there's also a white and a rosé), this red wine is a fantastically easy sipper, and has a rare low price for an Okanagan wine of this quality.

TRIVIA Latitude 50 degrees north is more or less where the Okanagan Valley (and Vancouver and Regina, too) fall on the globe.

PAIR WITH Pasta, chicken, pizza, barbecue or roast beast (game birds, too).

UNCORK For Canada Day celebrations, hump day, festive family gatherings, picnics, hot summer nights.

UNCORKED!

TINHORN CREEK

Tinhorn Creek

WINERY

Merlot   2008

VARIETY   YEAR

Okanagan Valley, B.C. $20

ORIGIN   PRICE   CLOSURE

The Okanagan Valley winemakers create some outstanding wines—but so often they sell for prices that are a wee bit beyond the reach of many of us, at least for everyday drinking. Not Tinhorn. One of the elder statesmen in the Canuck wine industry, Tinhorn makes a full range of wines that are 1) easy to find, 2) affordable, and 3) yummy. Like this Merlot. Winemaker Sandra Oldfield hails from California but has been making great wine at Tinhorn since the early days.

TRIVIA The winery's founder, Bob Shaunessy, is a Calgary engineer and co-founder of Trigger Resources. The winery's architect is Richard Lindseth, also a Calgarian; he designed the Calgary wine shop Kensington Wine Market.

PAIR WITH Beef, lamb, stew, cassoulet, lasagna, pasta with tomato sauce, cheese, even turkey or roast chicken.

UNCORK Now, for Canada Day, turkey day, the first day of winter, January cold spells, dinner with tourists.

MIKE WEIR WINE

Mike Weir Wine
WINERY

Pinot Noir   2007
VARIETY   YEAR

Niagara Peninsula, Ontario $17
ORIGIN   PRICE   CLOSURE

One for the golfers in the crowd. It would take an entire book to list all of Mike Weir's career highlights, so let's just say that Weir—aka Weirsy—is one of Canada's top golfers. He isn't a winemaker, but he is a fan of good wines, and a few years ago he was asked by the folks at Château des Charmes—one of Canada's finest wineries—if he'd consider making a wine. The rest, as the saying goes, is history. Proceeds from each bottle go to children's wellness across Canada via his charity, the Mike Weir Foundation.

TRIVIA The Niagara connection isn't random. Weir, who grew up in Ontario, spent a big part of his childhood in the Niagara region.

PAIR WITH Lamb, steak, hamburgers.

UNCORK After a day of golfing, meeting his/her parents for the first time.

UNCORKED!

NAKED GRAPE

Naked Grape		
WINERY		
unoaked Shiraz	Non-vintage	
VARIETY	YEAR	
Niagara Peninsula, Ontario	$10	
ORIGIN	PRICE	CLOSURE

The name "Naked Grape" might sound cheeky—and it is—but it also refers to the fact that this wine hasn't spent any time in oak barrels. In other words, you can actually taste the fruit that's used to make the wine. Wine snobs slam this one, but it sells. A lot. Take it for what it is: a very inexpensive wine (one of the cheapest in the book) that pleases crowds and goes down easily, and one you can find almost everywhere in the province.

TRIVIA Shiraz isn't just a grape. It's also the sixth-largest city in Iran.

This is not a VQA (Vintners Quality Alliance) wine; it can contain grapes from regions outside of Canada.

PAIR WITH Burgers, pizza, pasta, lasagna. Or drink by itself.

UNCORK For hump day (duh), NHL playoffs, frat parties, third dates, any time you need a red wine for cooking.

NO. 99 WAYNE GRETZKY ESTATES

No. 99 Wayne Gretzky Estates
....
WINERY

Cabernet Sauvignon–Merlot   2007
....
VARIETIES   YEAR

Niagara Peninsula, Ontario $19
....
ORIGIN   PRICE   CLOSURE

Yes, you read that correctly: Wayne Gretzky, the former Edmonton Oiler and, well, all-around hockey legend. These days, however, the Great One has become the Grape One. He teamed up with Niagara's Creekside Estate Winery to create the offshoot No. 99. Although Gretzky says he isn't much of a wine drinker, the winery gives him an opportunity to raise funds for his charity, the Wayne Gretzky Foundation, which helps kids who couldn't otherwise afford to play sports. As for the wine itself, it's a big, smooth blockbuster of a blend, good enough to please even a Calgary Flames fan or two.

TRIVIA Gretzky isn't especially involved in the winery's day-to-day operations—California, not Canada, is now his home. But on a promotional tour for the winery a year or so ago, he admitted that this blend is his favourite of all the No. 99 wines.

PAIR WITH Steak, roast beef, lamb, and hard Parmesan-style cheese.

UNCORK While watching *Hockey Night in Canada*, after you score a goal playing street hockey with your buds, any time you want to remind your friends that real men (and women, too) don't have to drink beer just because they like hockey. Drink now or cellar for up to four years.

UNCORKED!

VINELAND ESTATES WINERY

Vineland Estates Winery
....
WINERY

Cabernet Franc   2008
....
VARIETY   YEAR

Niagara Peninsula, Ontario $15.50
....
ORIGIN   PRICE   CLOSURE

This classic red wine comes from one of Niagara's star wineries—and one with a fairly lengthy history, at least by Canuck standards. Vineland is 25 years old, which practically makes it a granddaddy compared to many of its Canadian counterparts. It's headed up by two brothers, Alan Schmidt (the president) and Brian Schmidt (the vice-president and winemaker).

TRIVIA The Schmidts grew up in the Okanagan Valley, where their parents were involved in the early days of Sumac Ridge Estate Winery, one of the OK Valley's long-time stars.

PAIR WITH Pork chops, hamburgers, leg of lamb.

UNCORK At Sunday dinner or dinner with the in-laws, or share with overseas visitors.

V I N E L A N D
ESTATES WINERY

2008
CABERNET FRANC
VQA NIAGARA PENINSULA VQA

ESTABLISHED   WINEMAKER
1979

BERINGER

Beringer	Founders' Estate	
WINERY	WINE NAME	
Cabernet Sauvignon	2007	
VARIETY	YEAR	
Napa Valley, California	$18	
ORIGIN	PRICE	CLOSURE

Easy to find, easy to love. Sometimes that's all you want from a wine. This smooth, easy-drinking Cabernet Sauvignon is a winner every time; it's made by a female winemaker, Laurie Hook. Now owned by megacorporation Foster's, Beringer's winery roots span three centuries, dating back to 1876.

TRIVIA A protected oak tree on the Beringer estate called the "Leaning Oak" is now more than two hundred years old; it was alive when the Constitution of the United States of America was signed in 1787.

PAIR WITH Steak (of course), roast beef, aged white cheddar, short ribs, cassoulet, pork tenderloin, leg of lamb.

UNCORK For dinner with the in-laws, family get-togethers, any time you don't know what to take but someone says, "Just bring some red wine, honey."

CANNONBALL

Cannonball Wine Company
WINERY

Cabernet Sauvignon   2008
VARIETY   YEAR

Sonoma Coast, California $25
ORIGIN   PRICE   CLOSURE

According to the label, a cannonball "is the perfect symbol of freedom. Legs tucked beneath you, soaring through the air." Well, I don't think you'll turn into the wine lover's equivalent of a Cirque du Soleil performer when you drink this wine, but you will find a handsome, big red wine that's loaded with notes of chocolate, vanilla, and black cherries.

TRIVIA The winery has its own Facebook page; become a fan by searching for Cannonball Wines.

PAIR WITH Steak, roast beef, burgers, or venison.

UNCORK At barbecues, frat parties, any gathering with pirates. Or stick in the cellar for a couple of years. If you open it and the tannins are still a bit big for you, decant it or wait an hour or so to drink it.

FRONTIER RED

Fess Parker	Frontier Red	
WINERY	WINE NAME	
Syrah blend	Non-vintage	
VARIETY	YEAR	
Santa Barbara County, California	$19	
ORIGIN	PRICE	CLOSURE

Pour some in your glass—or, even better, decant it and *then* pour it into your glass. Wait a few minutes. Swirl it around a little and take a big sniff. A blend of mostly Syrah with a whole pile of other reds. Spice and fruit—and a great throbbing wallop of alcohol (15.5 percent, to be exact). Don't chugalug this one, even if you're tempted.

Eli Parker is the winemaker; he and his father, Fess, set out to start a small vineyard and sell the fruit to wineries. But, says Fess's daughter Ashley, "Fess is from Texas, so he can't do anything small."

TRIVIA Fess Parker, the guy who owned this winery till he died in early 2010, was 6 feet 6 inches (198 cm) tall. He was also the actor who played Daniel Boone in the 1960s, and, before that, he played Davy Crockett (in two of Disney's early live-action movies). King of the wild frontier, he was.

PAIR WITH Barbecue chicken or steak, ribs, grilled portobello mushroom caps.

UNCORK Now, on camping trips, or hanging out with actors and cowboys.

UNCORKED!

GALLO

Gallo Family Vineyards
WINERY
....

Merlot   2008
VARIETY   YEAR
....

Sonoma, California $9
ORIGIN   PRICE   CLOSURE
....

Maybe you're in a small town or you're in a rush or you're in an unfamiliar part of the city, and you just need to pick up a bottle of good red wine. Fast. Here's a reliable red for that occasion. The folks at Gallo make consistently delicious wines at very good prices, and they make a lot of wine, so no matter where you are, there's a good chance you can find a bottle.

TRIVIA Gallo Family Vineyards, which makes this wine, is the largest family-owned winery in the world. (It's been around for more than seventy-five years.)

PAIR WITH Lamb, steak, roast beef, roasted vegetables, tagine, beef stew.

UNCORK Now, family gatherings, hump day, camping trips, any time someone says, "Bring a red," but doesn't tell you what they're cooking.

GHOST PINES

Ghost Pines	Winemaker's Blend	
WINERY	WINE NAME	
Cabernet Sauvignon	2008	
VARIETY	YEAR	
Napa/Sonoma, California	$20	
ORIGIN	PRICE	CLOSURE

Maybe you believe in ghosts. Maybe you don't. But after trying this wine, you will believe in Ghost Pines and, for that matter, affordable, good vino from California. Made with grapes grown in both Napa Valley and Sonoma, this Cabernet Sauvignon is smooth, spicy, and berry delicious.

TRIVIA Depending on the type of tree they come from, pine cones can weigh close to ten pounds (that's about five kilos). Loggers used to call them "widow-makers" because one could kill you if it landed on your head.

PAIR WITH Steak, ribs, lamb.

UNCORK For camping trips, family get-togethers, the first time you cook for his/her parents. Decant it if you find it a bit too tannic; or stick it in your cellar for up to five years.

GNARLY HEAD

Gnarly Head	Old Vine Zin
WINERY	WINE NAME
Zinfandel	2008
VARIETY	YEAR
Lodi, California	$19
ORIGIN	PRICE	CLOSURE

The '70s rock band Creedence Clearwater Revival sang a song called "Lodi"—as in "Oh! Lord, stuck in Lodi again." Maybe back then winemakers in Lodi weren't cranking out good wine like they are today cuz if you have to be stuck somewhere, Lodi—the Zinfandel capital of North America—sure sounds like a pleasant place to be. Lodi is pronounced "LOW-die," just in case you were wondering.

TRIVIA The name "Gnarly Head" refers to how Zinfandel vines are pruned. After a few years, even generations, they get all curled up and knotty. Some of these vines are eighty years old. When I'm eighty, I want to be curled up and naughty, too. Naughty? Knotty? Or Gnarly Head? All may describe how you'll feel the next day if you drink too much of this stuff. Or any other booze, for that matter.

PAIR WITH Steak, barbecue, sausages, short ribs, wings, or drink by itself.

UNCORK Now, at backyard barbecues, NHL playoffs, camping trips, tailgate parties, family gatherings, picnics.

McMANIS

McManis Family Vineyards
....
WINERY

Merlot	2008
VARIETY	YEAR

San Joaquin County, California $19.50
....
ORIGIN   PRICE   CLOSURE

Fourth-generation farmers, the McManis family has been growing grapes since 1938, and in 1990, they decided to make wine. So far, so good; they've been racking up awards across the U.S., which is generally a pretty good sign. Even better? This wine, a smooth-as-silk red that's all berries and cocoa and deliciousness.

TRIVIA Linguists believe the word *Merlot* comes from an ancient French word for "young blackbirds." (Merlot berries are dark coloured. Bet the birds liked to eat 'em, too.)

PAIR WITH Lamb, steak, bison burgers, tagine, shawarma.

UNCORK For family gatherings, hump day, casual Friday nights with friends.

UNCORKED!

PURPLE COWBOY

Purple Cowboy	Tenacious Red	
WINERY	WINE NAME	
Cabernet Sauvignon–Syrah	2008	
VARIETIES	YEAR	
Paso Robles, California	$16	
ORIGIN	PRICE	CLOSURE

You won't need a horse or a hat or cowboy boots to drink this wine, but if you have 'em, you'll enjoy it that much more. This wine doesn't take itself too seriously (hence the cute name)—yet it's serious enough to be part of a good cause.

A tenacious gal and breast cancer survivor (and rodeo family member) named Terry Wheatley started this winery a couple of years ago. She's been working in the California wine industry for more than thirty years. A portion of Purple Cowboy sales goes toward Wheatley's charity, Tough Enough to Wear Pink, which raises money for cancer researchers around the world, including Canada.

TRIVIA Wheatley started her career as a teenager, working as a trick rider at events for Gallo Family Vineyards.

PAIR WITH Steak, burgers, ribs, roast, grilled vegetables.

UNCORK Now, for dinners with cowboys, Stampede parties, any time you need a party-hearty red. Or want to support a good cause.

RAVENSWOOD

Ravenswood	Vintners Blend
WINERY	WINE NAME
Zinfandel	2007
VARIETY	YEAR
Sonoma, California	$17
ORIGIN	PRICE

CLOSURE

The Ravenswood Winery specializes in Zinfandel, so it stands to reason that staff would do a good job of it. Although they make many different types of Zin, this entry-level (aka one of the most affordable) Zin is always reliable, easy to find, and so big and rich and tasty. Joel Peterson—who started the winery in the 1970s—gave Ravenswood its slogan: "No wimpy wines." You'll know why when you try this brash baby.

TRIVIA Diehard Ravenswood fans around the world take their dedication far beyond the glass; Peterson says he often meets people who have been tattooed with the winery's signature Celtic knot of three intertwined ravens.

PAIR WITH Barbecue, steak, roast beef, ribs, tagine, lamb, spicy Italian sausage. Or enjoy by itself.

UNCORK For tailgate parties, hot summer nights, NHL playoffs. Or stick in the cellar.

UNCORKED!

SEBASTIANI

Sebastiani	
WINERY	

mostly Zinfandel (see below)	2007	
VARIETY	YEAR	

Sonoma County, California	$20	
ORIGIN	PRICE	CLOSURE

Sounds Italian. Looks Italian. Comes from California. And while it says "Zinfandel" on the label, it contains a little bit of Malbec, Syrah, and Petite Sirah, too. Zinfandel can sometimes be a rough-and-ready party wine, the sort of thing to knock back quickly by a campfire. But this one's elegant. Classy, even. Tastes (and smells) like raspberries and a beautiful fall day in California.

TRIVIA Samuele Sebastiani—who started the winery in 1904—survived Prohibition (1920 to 1933, when no one in the U.S. could sell booze) by selling sacramental wine and turning the winery into a cannery.

PAIR WITH Sausages, steak, pizza, short ribs, wings. Or drink by itself.

UNCORK For family get-togethers, dinners with the boss, Friday night casual get-togethers, first dates, first snowfalls, meeting his/her parents for the first time. Or cellar for a year or two.

FIRESTEED

Firesteed
WINERY

Pinot Noir   2008
VARIETY   YEAR

Willamette Valley, Oregon $20
ORIGIN   PRICE   CLOSURE

When I was a kid, I bought a fiery black-and-white pinto horse from my uncle for $20. It took me a year to save up for her, and I never, ever learned to ride her. Not well, anyway. Eventually, my dad sold her to a friend, and she lived out her days fat and happy. I still think about her. You'll still think about this wine once you taste it. Despite the name, it's a mild-mannered, food-friendly red. As inexpensive as that long-ago horse, and a lot easier to handle.

TRIVIA The name "Firesteed" comes from the fact that fire (one of the four elements) is a symbol of passion, and horses symbolize strength and grace. And the wine? A little of all three, I guess.

PAIR WITH Cedar-planked salmon, grilled lamb.

UNCORK For camping trips, rodeos, romantic dinners.

WINE BY JOE

Wine By Joe
....
WINERY

Pinot Noir   2008
....
VARIETY   YEAR

Willamette Valley, Oregon $25
....
ORIGIN   PRICE   CLOSURE

The label says it all—down to earth, unpretentious wine that's really good. Sniff it, and you'll get aromas of cherries and blackberries, maybe a hint of leather. (I did, anyway, and I liked it.)

TRIVIA Looking for recipes to pair with this Pinot Noir? Go to winebyjoe.com.

PAIR WITH Grilled salmon, chicken, roast duck, wild boar (just in case you have some kickin' around), or mushroom risotto.

UNCORK Now; at hipster dinners; any time you need a "serious wine for the unserious," as it says at winebyjoe .com. Or "on the tailgate of your four-by-four truck at the monster truck rally." Indeed, there's a wine for every occasion.

THE VELVET DEVIL

Charles Smith Wines	The Velvet Devil	
WINERY	WINE NAME	
Merlot	2008	
VARIETY	YEAR	
Columbia Valley, Washington	$21	
ORIGIN	PRICE	CLOSURE

The bold (but somehow simple) black-and-white Charles Smith labels can't be missed. Then there are the names, like Kung Fu Girl Riesling (in homage to Lucy Liu's character in the movie *Kill Bill*) and Boom Boom! Syrah. But the wines aren't a joke. Not at all—Smith is one of the top winemakers in North America. The Velvet Devil Merlot smells like dark chocolate and vanilla. And it is, as you'd hope, as smooth as velvet.

TRIVIA Before he went into winemaking, Smith managed rock bands in Europe, including the Raveonettes and the Cardigans.

PAIR WITH Steak, lamb, any kind of red meat. Or try with turkey.

UNCORK For Halloween (duh), tailgate parties, turkey day, patio nights. And any time you want to stay up all night, drink too much, and feel like a rock star.

UNCORKED!

WATERBROOK

Waterbrook	Mélange Noir
WINERY	WINE NAME

red blend (see below)	2008
VARIETY	YEAR

Columbia Valley, Washington	$17.50	
ORIGIN	PRICE	CLOSURE

Located in the heart of Walla Walla, Washington (say that ten times fast), Waterbrook turns twenty-five years old this year; it was the fourth winery registered in the region. Now there are more than one hundred, and Waterbrook is still thriving.

Why? The wine says it all. This super-easy red is soft and smooth, a blend of Merlot, Cabernet Sauvignon, Sangiovese, Cabernet Franc, and a few mystery grapes thrown in for good measure.

TRIVIA One of the definitions of the First Nations term *Walla Walla* is "running water," which is where Waterbrook got its name.

PAIR WITH Think steak, lamb, shawarma, roast beef, pork loin, even turkey.

UNCORK Now; for large family gatherings; turkey day; any time someone says, "Bring a red," but doesn't tell you what they're serving; book clubs; hump day; any time you want a red wine.

CHATEAU D'ARGADENS

Chateau d'Argadens

....

WINERY

Merlot/Cabernet Sauvignon/Cabernet Franc   2007

....

VARIETIES   YEAR

Bordeaux, France $24

....

ORIGIN   PRICE   CLOSURE

A blend of Merlot and Cabernet Sauvignon (the top two red wine grapes of Bordeaux) and a little bit of Cabernet Franc, this easy-drinking red is an excellent introduction to Bordeaux wines, considered by hard-core wine snobs to be some of the world's greatest *vin*. The Sichel family, who own d'Argardens, also own Chateau Palmer and Château Margaux, two of the most famous estates in Bordeaux.

TRIVIA Brits call red Bordeaux "claret," which, if you're pronouncing it correctly, rhymes with "carrot."

PAIR WITH Beef, lamb, Camembert, brie.

UNCORK At dinner with wine snobs, dinner with the boss, dinner with Francophiles. Or cellar for a couple of years.

UNCORKED!

CHATEAU TIMBERLAY

Chateau Timberlay
....
WINERY

Merlot/Cabernet Sauvignon/Cabernet Franc   2007
....
VARIETIES   YEAR

Bordeaux, France $18
....
ORIGIN   PRICE   CLOSURE

Bordeaux may be the most complicated wine region in the world to understand. With that in mind, here is the Coles Notes version of this wine: it's a blend of Merlot and Cabernet Sauvignon, with a wee bit of Cabernet Franc thrown in.

Chateau Timberlay is owned by the family of Robert Giraud, who still live in the actual château on the estate. They also own several other major French estates.

TRIVIA Even the simplest, least-expensive Bordeaux wines are allowed to have the words *Grand Vin de Bordeaux* on the label.

PAIR WITH Steak, roast beef, grilled chicken, pheasant, Cornish game hen.

UNCORK For family gatherings, dinner with Francophiles, dinners with your English granny, any time you're feeling superior.

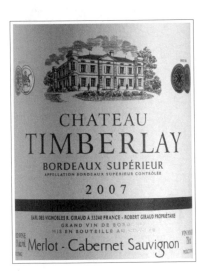

DOMAINE LAFAGE

Domaine Lafage	Cuvée Nicolas
WINERY	WINE NAME

Grenache Noir	2007
VARIETY	YEAR

Languedoc-Roussillon, France	$21	
ORIGIN	PRICE	CLOSURE

Domaine Lafage is a very young estate, started a few years ago by Jean-Marc Lafage and Eliane Salinas-Lafage (the winemaker), near Perpignan in southwest France by the border with Spain.

Cuvée Nicolas is light and subtle, with soft tannins, so you can drink it now as is, or you can cellar it for a year or two. Sure, it may sound like a cliché, but this wine is elegant with a capital *E*.

TRIVIA "Cuvée Nicolas" is named for the lively son of Jean-Marc and Eliane. The couple decided to make a special wine just for him because of "his patience" at waiting to be born until harvest was finished.

PAIR WITH Grilled Mediterranean vegetables, grilled chicken, even lamb tagine.

UNCORK For impressing a wine geek, barbecues, dinners with Francophiles.

UNCORKED!

DOMAINE PAUL AUTARD

Domaine Paul Autard
....
WINERY

Grenache-Syrah   2008
....
VARIETIES   YEAR

Côtes du Rhône, France $18
....
ORIGIN   PRICE   CLOSURE

You could write a book about nothing but French wines; tons of people have done just that. What you need to know: this wine is fresh and fruity, and meant to be drunk young, so even though it's French, you don't have to stick it in the cellar for 10 years. It's also a blend of mostly Grenache and Syrah, with a bit of Mourvèdre and Cinsault thrown into the mix.

TRIVIA *Côtes* literally means "slopes" or "hills," and the Rhône is one of France's most famous rivers. Put them together and you get one of the biggest wine-producing regions in France.

PAIR WITH French cheese, roast pork or beef, beef daube (aka stew), grilled chicken, and turkey.

UNCORK For turkey day, Sunday dinners, dinners with Francophiles. Or stick in the cellar for a year or two.

LA VIEILLE FERME

La Vieille Ferme
....
WINERY

Syrah/Cinsault/Mourvèdre/Carignan   2008
....
VARIETIES   YEAR

Côtes du Ventoux, France $14
....
ORIGIN   PRICE   CLOSURE

I see a chicken on a wine label and I immediately start to think about a nice roast chicken and a glass of wine on a Sunday night. Mmm . . . chicken. Here's a laid-back wine for those nights when you just feel like relaxing and hanging out and having a good time. For those of us who didn't take basic French in elementary school, *La Vieille Ferme* means "the old farm." But all you really need to know is *bon vin*: good wine.

TRIVIA This label was created by one Jean-Pierre Perrin, whose family also owns Château de Beaucastel, one of Châteauneuf-du-Pape's most famous estates.

PAIR WITH Grilled meat, cheese, Mediterranean dishes.

UNCORK For going home to the farm, family gatherings, January snowfalls, casual Friday nights, and Sunday dinners.

HOLD-UP

Rhône Gang	Hold-up
WINERY	WINE NAME
Pinot Noir–Grenache	2008 ("No. 8")
VARIETIES	YEAR
Rhône Valley, France	$18
ORIGIN	PRICE	CLOSURE

This may be a French wine, but there's something so very Albertan about the curly handlebar moustaches on the label. Then there's the name; it just smacks of stagecoaches and the Wild Wild West. From four creative young winemakers—all friends, all from different wineries—who decided to break with tradition and create a fun, completely unpretentious red blend.

TRIVIA Winemakers in the Rhône Valley produced 399 million bottles last year. Yes, you read that correctly.

PAIR WITH Burgers, cheese, lamb, steak, roasted veggies, oven-roasted potatoes, duck, chicken.

UNCORK For Stampede parties, rodeos, NHL playoffs, football games.

CASTELLO ROMITORIO

Castello Romitorio
....
WINERY

Sangiovese—Cabernet Sauvignon   Morellino di Scansano   2007
....
VARIETIES   WINE NAME   YEAR

Montalcino, Italy $21
....
ORIGIN   PRICE   CLOSURE

Castello Romitorio has been around since
the 12th century, but over time, it crumbled
into ruins. Then a rather famous Italian artist
named Sandro Chia bought the place in 1984.
(Keep the Chia Pet jokes to yourself.) He
had it restored, and then bought this property near Scansano, a beautiful little town in
Tuscany. Scansano is especially known for its
wine, Morellino di Scansano, and this is a fine

example of it, a dark
ruby-red blend of
Sangiovese (85 per-
cent) and Cabernet
Sauvignon (15 per-
cent). A great wine
for anyone who likes
Chianti.

TRIVIA *Morellino* means
"Sangiovese" in the local
Italian dialect.

PAIR WITH Grilled red
meats, including venison and
bison burgers, hard cheeses.

UNCORK Now, with artists,
Italophiles, and royalty.

FARNESE

Farnese		
WINERY		
Primitivo	2008	
VARIETY	YEAR	
Ortona, Italy	$13	
ORIGIN	PRICE	CLOSURE

All the wines in this book are a great value, or they wouldn't be here. But some cost very, very little money—but deliver in a very, very big way. This is one of those wines, a classic Italian Primitivo that you can get for the price of about two fancy coffee shop lattes.

TRIVIA In the 1500s, a princess by the name of Margherita of Austria married an Italian guy named Ottavio Farnese. A big fan of her adopted homeland, she made sure the royal courts of Europe had a steady supply of the wines of the region. And that's how Farnese began.

PAIR WITH Sausage, pizza, pasta with tomato sauce.

UNCORK Now, Friday night pizza parties, NHL playoffs, tailgate parties, watching reruns of *The Sopranos*.

FEUDI DI SAN GREGORIO

Feudi di San Gregorio
....
WINERY

Primitivo di Manduria   2008
....
VARIETY (AND APPELLATION)   YEAR

Puglia, Italy $20
....
ORIGIN   PRICE   CLOSURE

The Feudi di San Gregorio estate is located on some of the oldest wine-producing land in what is now Italy; records show that wine grapes were grown there as far back as AD 590. Yes, you read that correctly.

This is the first vintage in which the Primitivo has been branded to look like the rest of the Feudi di San Gregorio labels; if you find a 2007 in the market, it will look considerably different. Either way, enjoy.

TRIVIA Primitivo is the twelfth-most-common grape in Italy. Or so they say. It's also Italian for "Zinfandel." With that in mind, you can expect this Primitivo to be a big, earthy, food-friendly red.

PAIR WITH Italian sausages, meatball sandwiches, steak, short ribs.

UNCORK For NHL playoffs, dinners with Italophiles, dinners with wine geeks.

UNCORKED!

FEUDO DI SANTA TRESA

Feudo di Santa Tresa	Cerasuolo di Vittoria	
WINERY	WINE NAME	
Nero d'Avola–Frappato	2005	
VARIETIES	YEAR	
Sicily, Italy	$21.50	
ORIGIN	PRICE	CLOSURE

A very berry delicious red. The super-fragrant Cerasuolo di Vittoria wines from Sicily are light and soft and perfumed with cherries—great red wines for fans of white. If only someone could capture the aroma and turn it into a perfume.

Many consider the Cerasuolo from Feudo di Santa Tresa (literally "the house of Saint Teresa") to be one of Sicily's best, and like other Cerasuolos, it's made from Nero d'Avola and Frappato grapes. Think of it as Italy's answer to Beaujolais, a wine that's made to be drunk young.

TRIVIA Saint Teresa was a Carmelite nun who lived in the 1500s; she practised discalceation—which is just a fancy word that means she went barefoot for spiritual reasons. She obviously never visited Fort McMurray in January, where people wear shoes for practical reasons.

PAIR WITH Grilled red pepper and eggplant, grilled tuna. Or drink by itself.

UNCORK For warm summer nights on the patio, first dates. Serve slightly chilled. Drink now, or cellar for two or three years.

FONTANAFREDDA

Fontanafredda		
WINERY		
Barbera d'Alba	2008	
VARIETY (AND APPELLATION)	YEAR	
Piedmont, Italy	$15	
ORIGIN	PRICE	CLOSURE

I just like to say the word *Fontanafredda*. It reminds me of *Barbapapa*, a funny little French cartoon from the '70s that featured colourful blobby characters, all with names like Barbamama and Barbabravo.

Well, this wine is colourful, albeit not particularly cartoony. Fontanafredda is a winery in Piedmont, in northern Italy, and it's particularly known for its Barolo—massive red wines that cost a lot and can be cellared for years. This Barbera, however, is a little easier, more approachable, and considerably less expensive than your average Barolo.

TRIVIA The Fontanafredda estate was built on the hunting grounds of King Vittorio Emanuele II, the first king of Italy.

PAIR WITH Steak, roast beef, venison, pork loin, lamb, bison burgers, Italian cheese, cheddar.

UNCORK For Sunday dinners, family gatherings, any time someone says, "Bring a red," but doesn't tell you what they're making. Drink now or cellar for a couple of years.

IL LABIRINTO

Fattoria Poggerino	Il Labirinto	
WINERY	WINE NAME	
Sangiovese	2007	
VARIETY	YEAR	
Chianti, Italy	$23	
ORIGIN	PRICE	CLOSURE

You won't see the word organic on the label of this Italian red, but the winery owners all practise organic farming—no pesticides, no herbicides, etc. Don't think you're drinking some hippy-dippy *vino* though; Il Labirinto is made from 100 percent Sangiovese grapes and is complex, very food friendly, and a great candidate for the cellar.

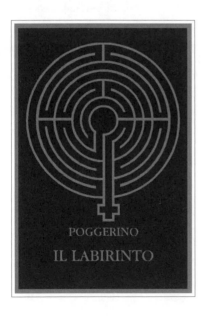

POGGERINO
IL LABIRINTO

TRIVIA The word *Sangiovese* comes from the Latin term *sanguis Jovis*, which literally means "the blood of Jove," aka Jupiter, the king of the gods and god of thunder. And labyrinths have been spiritually significant for millennia; walk into the heart of a labyrinth to find your inner self. Ponder that while you sip.

PAIR WITH Thin shards of hard Parmigiano Reggiano, Tuscan-style bread with salt and olive oil, Italian cured meats, risotto with mushrooms, grilled lamb.

UNCORK For dinner with wine snobs or organic-food fans. Or cellar for up to five years.

LAMURA

Lamura
....
WINERY

Nero d'Avola	Rosso di Sicilia	2009
VARIETY	WINE NAME	YEAR

Sicily, Italy	$14	
ORIGIN	PRICE	CLOSURE

Lamura is an offshoot of Casa Girelli, a winery located near Verona. Lamura, however, is in Sicily and their wines are made from Sicily's signature red wine grape, Nero d'Avola. This wine is an outstanding (and organic!) example of it. You'll get loads of soft tannins (the stuff that makes the inside of your mouth feel dry when you sip it), dark fruity notes, and glorious spice and herbal aromas—pepper, lavender, rosemary, and marjoram all come to mind.

TRIVIA *La mura* in dialect Italian means "the wall." Don't drink and drive, or you may hit *la mura.*

PAIR WITH Spicy Italian sausage, pizza, or tomato-based pasta dishes (lasagna, pasta puttanesca, you name it). Or drink by itself.

UNCORK On hot summer evenings, or nights when you wish you could hop on an airplane and get outta town.

UNCORKED!

MARITMA

Amanzio Tamanti	Maritma
WINERY	WINE NAME

Sangiovese	2008
VARIETY	YEAR

Maremma, Italy	$16	
ORIGIN	PRICE	CLOSURE

This 100 percent Sangiovese is sometimes referred to as the "four old guys" wine for, well, four old guys on the label. People have been drinking wine made from Sangiovese—central Italy's star grape—since the 16th century. So it too is also old. Very old. But don't think you have to be ancient to drink this pretty Sangiovese. Drink it (while you're) young. As in now.

TRIVIA This wine is made in Italy by a friendly guy named Amanzio Tamanti, a consulting winemaker who moved to San Francisco 17 years ago; he's still trying to figure out why he can walk down the street in the U.S. and buy an AK-47 but he has to put a health warning label on his wine, wine that he makes back home in Italy.

PAIR WITH Tomato-based pasta, pizza, Italian-style seafood.

UNCORK Now, at birthday parties for old men. Um, on second thought, try during Sophia Loren tribute nights, casual Fridays, hump day. And, well, birthday parties for old men.

MASI

Masi	Campofiorin
WINERY	WINE NAME
Corvina/Rondinella/Molinara	2007
VARIETIES	YEAR
Veneto, Italy	$22
ORIGIN	PRICE	CLOSURE

This big, richer-than-rich, velvety wine is positively lush, curvy, and full. Sophie Dahl, not Kate Moss. Or, if you're more old school, think of the voluptuous models for the painters Titian or Rubens, not some half-starved waif. Yes, this wine is the stuff of art. Some

people call it a "super Venetian"; others call it a "baby Amarone." Either way, it's made by passing a young wine over the partially dried skins left over from making Amarone. And although the process has been copied by many other wineries, Masi, so the story goes, did it first.

TRIVIA The name *Campofiorin* literally means "field of flowers."

PAIR WITH Pasta with Bolognese sauce, lasagna, slivers of Parmigiano Reggiano cheese.

UNCORK During January cold spells, *Godfather* movie nights, dinners with Italophiles. Or cellar for a few years.

NIPOZZANO

Marchesi de Frescobaldi	Nipozzano Riserva	
WINERY	WINE NAME	
mostly Sangiovese	2006	
VARIETY	YEAR	
Chianti Rufina, Italy	$22	
ORIGIN	PRICE	CLOSURE

The Frescobaldi family—Italian nobility—has been making wine in Italy's Tuscany region for more than seven hundred years. The Nipozzano estate is one of many that they own throughout Italy. The Chianti Rufina wine region is a little hillier and cooler than its sister region, Chianti Classico. Made mostly from Sangiovese, an incredibly food-friendly wine, this Nipozzano is plummy and big, all cinnamon and spice and everything nice.

TRIVIA The Frescobaldis supplied wine to King Henry VIII and Michelangelo, who traded his paintings for wine. No word on how many bottles per masterpiece.

PAIR WITH Hard cheese, steak, stew, bison burgers.

UNCORK Now, at barbecue nights, family gatherings, Friday night dinners. Or cellar for a few years.

PODERI DI LUIGI EINAUDI

Poderi di Luigi Einaudi
....
WINERY

Dolcetto di Dogliani   2008
....
VARIETY (AND APPELLATION)   YEAR

Piedmont, Italy $24
....
ORIGIN   PRICE   CLOSURE

If you like Italian wines, think of a Dolcetto as the soft kid sister to, say, a Barbera. The Barbera is older, bossier, maybe a little more highfalutin. But the Dolcetto? A quiet little gem of a kid in the background. She'll shine, if you give her a chance. But she needs food. No supermodel, this one, she wants her salami, her pasta, her lasagna, or even polenta.

The Luigi Einaudi winery—in northern Italy, close to the German and French borders—is renowned for being a top Dolcetto producer (as well as Barolo, if your pockets are deep).

TRIVIA Luigi Einaudi was Italy's first president; later, he started a winery. The word *Dolcetto* means "sweet little one" in Italian. But don't take it literally; this wine is dry, not sweet.

PAIR WITH Roast duck, cassoulet, grilled meat, home-made lasagna, pizza.

UNCORK Now, at dinners with Italophiles, big family gatherings, nights of *Sopranos* reruns on TV.

UNCORKED!

R

Alpha Zeta	R	
WINERY	WINE NAME	
Corvina-Rondinella	Valpolicella	2008
VARIETIES	APPELLATION	YEAR
Veneto, Italy	$20	
ORIGIN	PRICE	CLOSURE

From A to Z (get it? Alpha to Zeta?), this is a big, smoky, rich, dark wine that's just perfect for a cold winter night.

Sometimes referred to as a "baby Amarone," a Ripasso wine is made when the winemaker takes a young red wine and blends it ("repasses" it over) with the leftover grapes from the Amarone winemaking process, grapes that are first dried for two months.

TRIVIA The winery was started by David Gleave, who was born and raised in Toronto and then lived in Vancouver for a while in his early 20s. He's now the managing director for Liberty Wines in London, England. Alpha Zeta's winemaker? A New Zealander named Matt Thomson.

PAIR WITH Italian feasts, braised meats. *Delicioso!*

UNCORK For winter solstice gatherings; big stewy dinners with friends who think a big jammy Aussie Shiraz is the be-all and end-all. Or stick in the cellar for a few years.

SASYR

Rocca delle Macìe	Sasyr	
WINERY	WINE NAME	
Sangiovese-Syrah	2006	
VARIETIES	YEAR	
Tuscany, Italy	$17	
ORIGIN	PRICE	CLOSURE

Have you heard of a "super Tuscan"? I'm not talking about a really nice guy from central Italy. I'm talking about a trendy name given to wines—often stunningly expensive wines—from (big surprise here) Tuscany. They don't follow traditional Tuscan blending laws (maybe they have a grape that's not common to the region, for instance); you can spot them by the letters "IGT" or the words *Indicazione Geografica Tipica* on the label.

As for the Sasyr, the name is literally what it sounds like: "Sa" for Sangiovese, and "Syr" for Syrah, which is, of course, just another word for Shiraz.

TRIVIA Ever watched a spaghetti western? Italo Zingarelli, the guy who started Rocca delle Macìe, was one of their producers; one of his most famous was *They Call Me Trinity*.

PAIR WITH Grilled meats, hard cheeses, Italian sausages.

UNCORK For rodeo season; Ultimate Fighting Championship nights; any time you feel like drinking, shooting a pistol, wearing a cowboy hat, or riding off into the sunset.

UNCORKED!

SCURATI

Azienda Agricola Ceuso	Scurati	
WINERY	WINE NAME	
Nero d'Avola	2007	
VARIETY	YEAR	
Sicily, Italy	$25	
ORIGIN	PRICE	CLOSURE

Rustic, intense, earthy, spicy. There are a lot of adjectives that could be used to describe this big, red-black wine from Sicily, one of the islands off the southern Italian coast. One for anyone who likes Shiraz, but wants to bust out and try something new.

TRIVIA *Nero d'Avola* literally means the "black of Avola," Avola being a city in Sicily and black referring to the dark colour of the grape.

PAIR WITH Lamb, pasta with meat sauce, lasagna, cured Italian meat, olives.

UNCORK Now, with wine geeks and carnivores. Or cellar for up to five years.

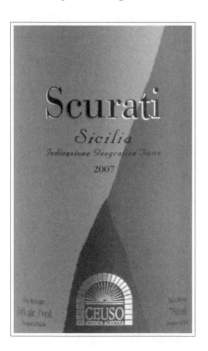

ZENATO

Zenato	Ripassa	
WINERY	WINE NAME	
Corvina/Rondinella/Sangiovese	Valpolicella	2007
VARIETIES	APPELLATION	YEAR
Veneto, Italy	$25	
ORIGIN	PRICE	CLOSURE

I never met the late Sergio Zenato, the guy who started the Zenato estate in 1960, but I think I would have liked him. People who knew him speak fondly of his joie de vivre, and his love of good food and wine. Ah, yes, wine. Like this curvy, full-bodied red. Imagine *Mad Men* star Christina Hendricks as a wine. Not only do the guys like her, but women want to be her friend, too. Classy and rich. Well dressed but not stuffy.

TRIVIA Made in the Ripasso style (the young wine spends some time with what's left from making Amarone), this wine's made from Corvina Veronese, Rondinella, and Sangiovese grapes.

PAIR WITH Italian feasts, braised meats (aka stews).

UNCORK During first snowfalls, January blizzards, spring storms, dinners with Italophiles. Or stick in the cellar for up to five years.

CASTILLO DE ALMANSA RESERVA

Bodegas Piqueras	Castillo de Almansa Reserva
WINERY	WINE NAME

Tempranillo/Monastrell/Garnacha	2006
VARIETIES	YEAR

Almansa, Spain	$12	
ORIGIN	PRICE	CLOSURE

Drink this wine and pretend you're in Spain. Made from three Spanish grape varieties (Tempranillo, Monastrell, and Garnacha [aka Grenache]), this easy-going sipper is often one of the province's best bargains when it comes to wine. Shop around. Then open any time you just want a glass of deep, dark, spicy, herbal, berry-ish red wine. It's also great for making sangria.

TRIVIA The castle on the label is real. Considered to be one of Spain's most beautiful, it is located in the town of Almansa, and it dates back to the 14th century.

PAIR WITH Roast beast, lasagna, paella.

UNCORK For hump day, casual family gatherings, NHL playoffs, tailgate parties.

CASTILLO DE MONSÉRAN

Castillo de Monséran
WINERY

old vine Garnacha | 2008
VARIETY | YEAR

Cariñena, Spain | $10
ORIGIN | PRICE | CLOSURE

This spicy red from Spain is a phenomenal deal (with one of the lowest prices in the book) and has won some impressive awards, too. It's a frequent hump-day wine at our house, one to open on weeknights when we come home from work and we just want a food-friendly wine that we don't have to think a lot about.

TRIVIA Garnacha is just another name for Grenache, the grape that the wine is made from.

PAIR WITH Pizza, lasagna, steak, hearty pasta dishes, chicken (cooked in myriad styles), frittatas, even cassoulet. Or mix with oranges and limes, triple sec, and sparkling water to make sangria.

UNCORK For hump day, family get-togethers, Grey Cup parties, NHL playoffs, tax season.

CUATRO PASOS

Bodegas Martín Códax	Cuatro Pasos
WINERY	WINE NAME
Mencia	2007
VARIETY	YEAR
Bierzo, Spain	$19
ORIGIN	PRICE

CLOSURE

Mencia—also known as Jaen—is the grape in this wine, and it's not exactly famous. Well, not outside of Spain, anyway. But it makes for interesting, good red wines; in fact, Bierzo, in northwest Spain, is one of country's newest, trendiest wine regions. I'm not the only person saying that. Really. This dusty, earthy, slightly flowery red wine rocks its own very unique style, and tastes just like where it comes from.

TRIVIA *Cuatro Pasos* means "four steps" in Spanish. Think of it as four steps in the right direction, toward red-wine bliss.

PAIR WITH Lamb, venison, sausage, fire-grilled peppers and eggplant and zucchini, chicken with olives.

UNCORK Now, with wine geeks, the fashion crowd, any time you need to take a new step forward. Or four.

DEHESA GAGO

Dehesa Gago	g	
WINERY	WINE NAME	
Tinta de Toro	2008	
VARIETY	YEAR	
Toro, Spain	$18.50	
ORIGIN	PRICE	CLOSURE

What you'll remember most about this bottle is the label: black, with a white lower-case *g*. For Gago, I assume. The grape here is Tinta de Toro, which wine pros generally say is another name for Tempranillo, one of Spain's most popular grapes. Despite being known as "Baby g" for the label, the wine is rather ballsy. Like a bull. Y'know, *toro*.

TRIVIA *Toro* also refers to one of Spain's up-and-coming wine regions, located north-west of Madrid near the border with Portugal. You're now one step ahead of the wine geeks, darlin'.

PAIR WITH Beef, lamb dishes, pork roast.

UNCORK For dinners with wine geeks, bullfights, Ultimate Fighting Championships (the closest thing we have to bullfights), rodeos, barbecues. Or cellar for a few years.

FINCA RESALSO

Bodegas Emilio Moro	Finca Resalso	
WINERY	WINE NAME	
Tempranillo	2007	
VARIETY	YEAR	
Ribera del Duero, Spain	$24	
ORIGIN	PRICE	CLOSURE

The thing about Tempranillo wines—and this one is made from 100 percent Tempranillo—is that they originated in places where food is paramount and, when it comes to popularity, wine isn't that far behind. In other words, Tempranillo (known as "Tinto Fino" in the Ribera del Duero region) is a slam dunk when it comes to pairing because it goes with all kinds of comestibles (especially meats), from lamb to roast duck to chicken souvlaki.

TRIVIA Finca Resalso was the winery's first vineyard, planted in 1932, the year that Emilio Moro (yes, there's a real person by that name) was born.

PAIR WITH Medium-rare steak, cured meat, olives (not the kind from a can), slow-roasted lamb.

UNCORK For NHL playoffs, major football games, tailgate parties, casual Friday night gatherings, dinners with wine geeks.

GABA DO XIL

Telmo Rodríguez	Gaba do Xil	
WINERY	WINE NAME	
Mencia	2008	
VARIETY	YEAR	
Valdeorras, Spain	$19	
ORIGIN	PRICE	CLOSURE

If you like red wine, you'll probably enjoy this velvety, smooth, rich red from Spain. And if you're a wine geek? You'll be in heaven. The winemaker here is Telmo Rodríguez, and he's one of Spain's young guns, a guy who's being watched by industry types around the world these days. He's big into using unusual grapes in out-of-the-way wine-producing regions of Spain, and this one's no exception; it's made from Mencia grapes, a type of Spanish grape that makes very fragrant, lighter-coloured (but still red!) wines.

TRIVIA Telmo Rodríguez is often called "the driving wine-maker" because he spends a lot of time just driving around in Spain, looking for neglected wine regions and vineyards that he can fix up.

PAIR WITH Roast leg of lamb, pork chops, cured meat, steak.

UNCORK At dinners with wine geeks, or at family get-togethers (bridging the family gap—note the bridges on the label!). Or cellar for a few years and see where Mr. Rodríguez's career takes him.

Gaba do Xil

MENCÍA
2008

VALDEORRAS
DENOMINACIÓN DE ORIGEN

HÉCULA

Bodegas Castaño	Hécula
WINERY	WINE NAME
Monastrell	2006
VARIETY	YEAR
Yecla, Spain	$16
ORIGIN	PRICE

CLOSURE

This dark purple wine is made from Monastrell grapes, aka Mourvèdre, aka Mataro. The vines are old. Well, at least forty years old—which is rather ancient if you're a vine. As they get older, the vines produce fewer grapes, but winemakers believe that's a good thing: those fewer grapes are considered to have more flavour. And, as any wine lover knows, flavour is good.

TRIVIA Yecla is a wine region located in eastern Spain, and Spain has more land planted to grapes than any other country in the world.

PAIR WITH Pizza, bison burgers, roast chicken, lamb.

UNCORK Now, at tailgate parties, casual dinner parties, fortieth-birthday parties, to meet his/her folks for the first time, just for the Hécula of it. Or cellar for a year or two.

L

Bodegas Castaño	Lujuria
WINERY	WINE NAME
Monastrell-Merlot	2006
VARIETIES	YEAR
Yecla, Spain	$11.50
ORIGIN	PRICE

CLOSURE

This label is so pretty and simple (designed by Vancouver's Jennifer Delf, a self-described bird lover and the wine's importer), maybe you'll underestimate the wine within the bottle. But it's delish. A blend of Monastrell (aka Mourvèdre) and Merlot, this easy-drinking red wine has smoky, fruity notes and nice, soft tannins, so drink it now. I am.

TRIVIA Google "lujuria" and you'll find . . . Well, on second thought, you may just want to know that the word *lujuria* means "lust" in Spanish. You might lust after this wine once you try a glass or two.

PAIR WITH Grilled meats (even roast chicken), paella, mild Italian sausages.

UNCORK For first dates, third dates, hot summer evenings, stag nights, hump nights, January snowstorms.

UNCORKED!

LAS ROCAS

Bodegas de San Alejandro	Las Rocas	
WINERY	WINE NAME	
Garnacha	2007	
VARIETY	YEAR	
Calatayud, Spain	$16	
ORIGIN	PRICE	CLOSURE

This spicy, dark purple wine is a great value. Not only does it come from ancient vines (sixty to eighty years old), it's made from Garnacha (aka Grenache or Alicante) grapes, which means it's very food friendly and accessible. One to turn into sangria (a fruity, boozy Spanish punch) or enjoy as is. A total deal.

TRIVIA *Las Rocas* literally means "the rocks." Think of this as a rock-star wine at a bargain-basement price.

PAIR WITH Steak, cured meat, spicy Italian sausage.

UNCORK Now, for camping trips, casual family gatherings, NHL playoffs, football games.

LA VENDIMIA

Palacios Remondo	La Vendimia	
WINERY	WINE NAME	
Tempranillo-Garnacha	2009	
VARIETIES	YEAR	
La Rioja, Spain	$19	
ORIGIN	PRICE	CLOSURE

All flash and no substance? Nope. The very pretty label—a colourful, stylized tree—may make you wonder if the Rioja inside the bottle is, in fact, as good. But it is; it's a stylish, elegant, fruit-packed spicy wine that's great to impress a wine snob, if you don't want to cough up for a pricier bottle. It's made from Tempranillo and Garnacha grapes.

TRIVIA Winemaker Alvaro Palacios is one of Spain's stars. He made his name with a (considerably more expensive) wine called "L'Ermita." And *Vendimia* is Spanish for "grape harvest" or "vintage."

PAIR WITH Pizza, charcuterie (aka cured meats), hard aged cheddar, Parmesan-style cheeses.

UNCORK At book club with your best gal pals, dinner with the boss, dinner with wine snobs.

UNCORKED!

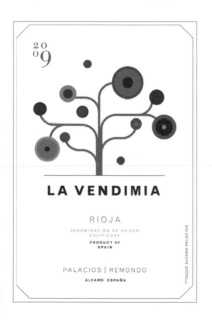

20 09

LA VENDIMIA

RIOJA

DENOMINACIÓN DE ORIGEN CALIFICADA

PRODUCT OF SPAIN

PALACIOS | REMONDO

ALFARO ESPAÑA

ALVARO PALACIOS

TRILOGÍA

Bodegas Los Frailes	Trilogía
WINERY	WINE NAME

Monastrell/Cabernet Sauvignon/Tempranillo	2006
VARIETIES	YEAR

Valencia, Spain	$23	
ORIGIN	PRICE	CLOSURE

The Los Frailes winery has been family owned since 1771, which is highly unusual. So's the wine, but also in a good way. This 100 percent organic blend of Tempranillo, Cabernet Sauvignon, and Monastrell (the region's main variety) is big and dark, spicy and juicy—and it excels with food.

TRIVIA More than two centuries ago, the land that belongs to this winery belonged to a group of Jesuit friars who were kicked out of Spain by the king in 1767. Four years later, ancestors of the family that now owns the winery bought it, hence the name Bodegas Los Frailes ("the friars' house").

PAIR WITH Hard (old) cheese, lamb, game, any kind of red meat.

UNCORK At dinner with organic-wine fans, dinner with the family priest.

CRASTO

Quinta do Crasto	Crasto
WINERY	WINE NAME

red blend (see below)	2007
VARIETY	YEAR

Douro Valley, Portugal	$19	
ORIGIN	PRICE	CLOSURE

You may not recognize any of the grapes that have made this wine, but you'll recognize the taste: good. Really, that one word says it all. As for the grapes? They're all indigenous Portuguese grapes, a mighty, earthy blend of Tinta Roriz, Tinta Barroca, Touriga Franca, and Touriga Nacional (Portugal's national grape, as some call it, and a main grape in making port). A slightly earthy red that goes down very easily.

TRIVIA The name *Crasto* comes from the Latin word meaning "Roman fort." Incidentally, winery staff still practise foot treading to squish the grapes. Yes, they stomp on the grapes to squeeze out the juice before turning the grapes into wine. Old school. Good.

PAIR WITH Grilled chicken, red wine–braised lamb shank.

UNCORK For casual Friday get-togethers, hump day, any time you want the little guy to win.

UNCORKED!

LUIS PATO

Luis Pato	Casta Baga
WINERY	WINE NAME
Baga	2005
VARIETY	YEAR
Bairrada, Portugal	$22	CLOSURE
ORIGIN	PRICE	

There really is a man named Luis Pato, whose family owns the winery; his daughter, Filipa, shares the winemaking responsibilities with her father. Baga is one of Portugal's most popular grapes and is especially common in the Bairrada region. This easygoing red isn't too big or heavy, but it's not a pushover, either. Think of it as a middleweight boxing champ, the kind of vino that can hold its own under all kinds of circumstances.

TRIVIA The word *pato* apparently means "duck" (as in "quack quack") in Portuguese, which explains the teeny picture of the quacker on the label.

PAIR WITH Grilled meat (chicken, beef, you name it), and, instead of a typical white wine, try with fish, such as salmon.

UNCORK For book clubs, Friday night dinners, first dates. Or cellar for a year or two.

PERIQUITA

José Maria da Fonseca	Periquita
WINERY	WINE NAME
Castelão	2007
VARIETY	YEAR
Portugal	$11
ORIGIN	PRICE
	CLOSURE

This wine has been made for more than 175 years, and even the label hasn't changed much over time. That is a pretty good inkling that what's inside the bottle is reliable, as well as aromatic, spicy, and herbal. The real José Maria da Fonseca was born in 1804, and the company that bears his name is Portugal's largest producer of table wines.

TRIVIA Not only is "Periquita" the name of this wine, it's also the name of the grape—aka Castelão—that's used to make it; it can also be used to make white and rosé wines. The word comes from the Portuguese word for parakeet.

PAIR WITH Steak, lamb, cheese. Or drink by itself.

UNCORK For Friday nights, hump day, book clubs, any time someone says, "Bring a bottle of red wine," but doesn't tell you what they're making. Or stick in the cellar for a few years.

DOMAINE MERCOURI

Mercouri Estate	Domaine Mercouri	
WINERY	WINE NAME	
Refosco-Mavrodaphne	2008	
VARIETIES	YEAR	
Letrina, Greece	$25	
ORIGIN	PRICE	CLOSURE

The Greeks have been making wine for, oh, thousands of years, but too many people still associate Greek wines with retsina, an unusual white that tastes like pine sap. This modern red couldn't be further from that style; it's a blend of Refosco (an Italian grape that makes big, full-bodied wines) and Mavrodaphne, one of Letrina's regional grapes.

TRIVIA Mercouri is located near the village of Korako-chori, which means "the place of the crow."

PAIR WITH Grilled lamb, pork roast, chicken, lasagna, hard cheese.

UNCORK For dinners with wine geeks, family gatherings, hump day, casual gatherings with friends. Or cellar for up to five years.

TSANTALI

Tsantali		
WINERY		

organic Cabernet Sauvignon	2006	
VARIETY	YEAR	

Halkidiki, Greece	$20	
ORIGIN	PRICE	CLOSURE

For more than one hundred years, this family-owned winery has been cranking out the good stuff (retsina, too, that pine-resin wine that people either love or hate). But Cabernet Sauvignon? Not exactly a typical Greek grape.

You'll want to break with tradition, too, when you sample this incredibly fragrant Cabernet. It's so herbal, so berry, so spicy; typical, yet not; one that clearly shows the terroir (the earth and water and climate) where it is produced.

CABERNET SAUVIGNON
Organic
FROM ORGANICALLY GROWN GRAPES   GREECE
TSANTALI

TRIVIA Tsantali is located in Halkidiki, Macedonia, in northwest Greece. Halkidiki was also the birthplace of Aristotle, one of the world's most famous philosophers. Funny quote from him: "Boys should abstain from all use of wine until their eighteenth year, for it is wrong to add fire to fire." One reason to keep the good stuff for the grown-ups.

PAIR WITH Roast leg of lamb with mustard and rosemary, souvlaki.

UNCORK At tailgate parties, cram sessions for astrophysics exams (it's all Greek to me.)

UNCORKED!

GALIL MOUNTAIN

Galil Mountain		
WINERY		

Cabernet Sauvignon	2008	
VARIETY	YEAR	

Israel	$16	
ORIGIN	PRICE	CLOSURE

Most Canucks probably don't typically think of Israel as being a hotbed for world-class wine, but, in fact, there have been some major award winners coming out of the tiny country in the past decade or so. The only problem? Most of the wineries are so small we don't get many, if any, of the bottles in Canada. Galil Mountain is an exception, and the wine? Exceptional—a big, bold, tannic Cabernet Sauvignon.

TRIVIA This wine is not just kosher; it's kosher for Passover, meaning it can be served during this major Jewish holiday.

PAIR WITH Steak, roast beef, roasted eggplant and red pepper.

UNCORK Now, at dinner with wine geeks, Passover, during barbecue season. Or cellar for up to five years.

GLEN CARLOU

Glen Carlou	Grand Classique
WINERY	WINE NAME
Cabernet Sauvignon–Merlot	2005
VARIETIES	YEAR
Paarl, South Africa	$17
ORIGIN	PRICE	CLOSURE

This beauty will make any red-wine fan happy—at least until the bottle's empty. Glen Carlou may sound like the name of an obscure Scotch, but it isn't; rather, it's a big, elegant red wine, all smoke and black currant and chocolate and vanilla and leather. Sound weird? Not once you give it a try. One for fans of French Bordeaux, it may convince them to look beyond the Old World when they're searching for fine wine.

TRIVIA Glen Carlou is owned by Hess Family Estates, a fourth-generation Swiss company that owns a handful of major wine properties around the world.

PAIR WITH A big, juicy steak, or drink by itself.

UNCORK Now, for third-date night, dinner with Francophiles, dinner with the boss.

Grand Classique 2005
cabernet sauvignon/merlot
wine of origin paarl

GLEN CARLOU

The handcrafted wines of David Finlayson

GOATS DO ROAM

Goats do Roam Wine Company		
WINERY		

Rhône blend (see below)	2008	
VARIETY	YEAR	

Paarl, South Africa	$14	
ORIGIN	PRICE	CLOSURE

If you don't drink French wine, you may not understand this rather punny name, a play on the classic French Côtes du Rhône region. (They also make one called "Bored Doe." Get it?) The wine at hand is made from classic Rhône grapes: Syrah, Cinsault, Carignan, Grenache, and Mourvèdre. Not too tannic, lots of red fruit. Yummy.

TRIVIA Goats do Roam Wine Company is the kid sister to Fairview, a much older (and, some would say, more serious) winery in South Africa. Wine has been made on the Fairview property (different moniker, same land) since the late 1600s.

PAIR WITH Chicken or lamb tagine, roast chicken, steak, or pot roast.

UNCORK For hump day, casual Friday gatherings, book clubs.

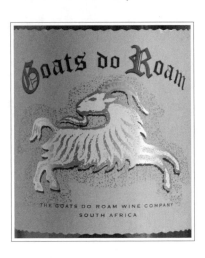

SEBEKA

Sebeka

WINERY

Cabernet Sauvignon–Pinotage   2008

VARIETIES   YEAR

Western Cape, South Africa $14

ORIGIN   PRICE   CLOSURE

I served a fancy-schmancy Bordeaux one year at a family gathering. It cost a mint and, well, I thought it was pretty good—until the friend with the Sebeka showed up. My relatives all deserted the Bordeaux in favour of the cheap-and-cheerful red blend from South Africa. They loved it—a chocolatey, spicy, smoky, earthy red blend—and by the end of the night, I was drinking it, too. (If you like it, you'll also want to try the Shiraz-Pinotage blend.)

TRIVIA Pinotage is South Africa's signature red wine grape and is a cross between Pinot Noir and Cinsault. In South Africa, Cinsault is known as Hermitage. Hence the name *Pinotage*—a mix of Pinot and Hermitage.

PAIR WITH Lasagna, grilled meats and vegetables, pizza.

UNCORK Now, around a campfire, at large family gatherings, on cold winter nights, any time someone says, "Bring a red," but doesn't tell you what they're serving.

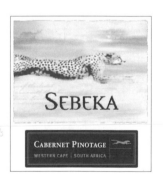

UNCORKED!

THE WOLFTRAP

Boekenhoutskloof	The Wolftrap	
WINERY	WINE NAME	
Syrah/Mourvèdre/Viognier	2008	
VARIETIES	YEAR	
Western Cape, South Africa	$13	
ORIGIN	PRICE	CLOSURE

Just the vino for when you need a big, bold blast; you'll want to open it on a first date with a bad boy, the kind of guy you won't want to take home to Mama but who you'll never forget. Oh my. This spicy blockbuster blend—Syrah, Mourvèdre, and Viognier—delivers a wallop of smoke, vanilla, chocolate, berries, and did I mention spice? Once or twice, I guess.

TRIVIA No wolf, real or otherwise, has ever been captured or, for that matter, even seen in the valley at Boekenhoutskloof, where this wine was made. There is, however, a 250-year-old trap. Just in case.

PAIR WITH Barbecue, tagine, ribs, pizza, burgers, bison, venison. Or enjoy by itself.

UNCORK For NHL playoffs, tailgate parties, barbecues, January nights, the first snowfall of the season. Or when entertaining boys named Peter (joke!).

SATELLITE

Satellite		
WINERY		

Pinot Noir	2008	
VARIETY	YEAR	

Marlborough, New Zealand	$22	
ORIGIN	PRICE	CLOSURE

Lou Reed used to sing a song called "Satellite of Love"—maybe that's what you'll be if you open a bottle of this fine red for your friends. (If you like it, and you like whites, too, search out the Satellite Sauvignon Blanc. Also fantastic.)

TRIVIA From the folks who have given us Spy Valley Wines, the names come from a spy base (with satellites— the kind that go into space, not the kind you drink) located near the winery. No Cold War here, however; you'll want this wine once you taste it.

PAIR WITH Pork loin, lamb, roast chicken, salmon.

UNCORK Now, for book club, dinner with the boss, a casual Friday night.

UNCORKED!

THE BLACK CHOOK

Woop Woop Wines	The Black Chook
WINERY	WINE NAME
Shiraz-Viognier	2008
VARIETIES	YEAR
McLaren Vale, South Australia	$18
ORIGIN	PRICE	CLOSURE

What's not to love about a wine that comes from Woop Woop? Apparently that's Aussie slang for the middle of nowhere . . . as in, "I've just been to Woop Woop and back." You're now thinking this might be the perfect wine for the next family reunion in Saskatchewan. But Woop Woop actually refers to a collaboration between a winemaker and a winery owner in South Australia, and while Woop Woop is its own label, the Black Chook is a sort of sister label, made in the same place.

Birds of a feather, flocking together.

Shiraz, of course, needs no introduction to most Canuck wine drinkers; it's big, spicy, dark, and delicious. And a tiny bit of Viognier—a white wine grape—is added to give a delicious, flowery apricot aroma to the blend. Lovely.

TRIVIA It won't come as a surprise, once you notice the big bird on the label, that *chook* is Aussie slang for "chicken."

PAIR WITH Barbecue, pizza, Cajun dishes, tagines. Or drink as is.

UNCORK For family get-togethers, backyard barbecues, Grey Cup parties, frat parties, tailgate parties, NHL playoffs, any time you need to, um, "Woop Woop" it up.

BLACK CYPRESS

Yarraman Estate	Black Cypress
WINERY	WINE NAME

Chambourcin	2008	$14.50
VARIETY	YEAR	PRICE

Hunter Valley, South Eastern Australia	
ORIGIN	CLOSURE

Australia is not exactly uncharted territory for fantastic wines, but this grape is definitely quirky. Chambourcin is a French-American hybrid grape that produces lovely, elegant, plummy smoky red wines, with an aromatic hit of black cherries.

Like many wines in this book, the grapes have all been hand-picked, which typically means the winemaker 1) has money and/or 2) is completely dedicated to quality. That may or may not be true, but either way, it gives you insider knowledge for your dinners with cork-dork friends.

TRIVIA The Yarraman vineyards were established in the 1950s by the late Max Schubert, one of the guys who put Penfolds on the map. And the Black Cypress reference? It's a type of tree found only in Australia.

PAIR WITH A variety of foods: this wine will be equally at home with red meats (game, steak), cassoulet-style dishes, or even lasagna. And some people swear by the combination of Chambourcin and dark chocolate.

UNCORK At dinner with wine geeks or with the boss.

BLEASDALE

Bleasdale	Second Innings	
WINERY	WINE NAME	

Malbec	2008	$14
VARIETY	YEAR	PRICE

Langhorne Creek, South Australia	
ORIGIN	CLOSURE

Malbec isn't exactly a grape that's typical in Australia, but this Bleasdale number proves not only that it's possible to grow Malbec in Oz, it can excel as a robust, macho, spicy red wine. Macho, but approachable: the soft, smooth tannins mean this wine's ready to drink now.

The Bleasdale winery was started by one Frank Potts in the late 1850s; he apparently liked to build things, all kinds of things, and

had a reputation as a bit of an eccentric, albeit one with a sense of humour. He named the winery after a teetotalling priest in his 'hood, and he made his own coffin, which he kept under his bed, filled with apples, until he died.

TRIVIA What, the coffin stuff wasn't enough for you? Here's more: "Second Innings" is a cricket term, a nod to family cricket games on their estate.

PAIR WITH Steak or barbecued meat.

UNCORK At barbecues, Grey Cup parties, cricket games. Drink now or cellar until 2012 or so.

DIGGERS BLUFF

Diggers Bluff	Stray Dog
WINERY	WINE NAME
Grenache/Shiraz/Mataro (GSM)	2006
VARIETIES	YEAR
Barossa Valley, Australia	$24
ORIGIN	PRICE

CLOSURE

Despite the cute name, this wine is created from one of the world's classic grape combinations: Grenache, Shiraz, and Mataro. Mataro is a grape that's usually called Mourvèdre, and, combined with Grenache and Shiraz, is often abbreviated as GSM in Australia. Although Diggers Bluff hails from Down Under, GSM can be found in France, where it appears in some Southern Rhône wines, especially Châteauneuf-du-Pape.

TRIVIA Tim O'Callaghan, the winemaker, named the winery for his pet, "the world's greatest dog." As for the bluff? It's where they live, overlooking a vineyard.

PAIR WITH Tagine, shawarma, Italian sausages, cured meats, roast or barbecue duck.

UNCORK For dog day afternoons, barbecues, family get-togethers.

UNCORKED!

LAYER CAKE

Layer Cake		
WINERY		
Shiraz	2009	
VARIETY	YEAR	
South Australia	$25	
ORIGIN	PRICE	CLOSURE

If you were rich and talented and loved to travel, maybe you'd follow your passion for wine, like Jayson Woodbridge, the guy behind Layer Cake Wines. He travels to the world's great wine regions, spends some time hanging out, and makes a fantastic wine—and then he moves on. Layer Cake Cabernet Sauvignon in Napa Valley, California. Malbec in Mendoza, Argentina. Primitivo in Puglia, Italy. (Are you jealous yet? Me too.) Oh yes, and this rich, dark fruit–bomb of a Shiraz, from Australia. It's all plums and cherries and chocolate and cigars. Devour it—just like a layer cake.

TRIVIA Woodbridge grew up in southern Ontario, then became an investment banker. When he realized he didn't want to have that career for the rest of his life, he saved his money and retired at the ripe (young) age of 35. Then he set his sights on wine.

PAIR WITH Chili, beef stew, short ribs, pizza, steak.

UNCORK For tailgate parties, book clubs, family gatherings, as a present for your investment banker.

JIP JIP ROCKS

Jip Jip Rocks
....
WINERY

Shiraz–Cabernet Sauvignon   2008
....
VARIETIES   YEAR

Padthaway, Limestone Coast,
Australia $19
....
ORIGIN   PRICE   CLOSURE

The Jip Jip Rocks are real, an outcropping of granite more than 350 million years old. Sacred to the Australian aboriginals, the rocks are located on the Limestone Coast, a historic whaling port and a major location for rock lobster fishing. As for the wine? Not so old. But it's delicious—a dark purple blend that's all cherries and licorice and spice. Mmm.

The family who owns this winery has been farming the same land for more than 150 years; nowadays they focus on wine, but they still raise cattle and other livestock, too.

TRIVIA Former Calgarian Brad Rey works in sales and marketing at the winery, as well as on several other Australian wine projects. Although he studied architecture at the University of Calgary, he holds a wine-making degree from Charles Sturt (no, that's not a typo) University in Australia.

PAIR WITH Roast beef, ribs, steak, tagine, stew, chili. Or drink by itself.

UNCORK Now, around a campfire, on cold winter nights, any time you find yourself surfing Expedia.ca and dreaming of distant lands, big rocks . . . and good wine.

UNCORKED!

JIP JIP ROCKS

SHIRAZ CABERNET

Padthaway - Australia
Family Owned - Estate Grown

PETER LEHMANN

Peter Lehmann of the Barossa	Layers
WINERY	WINE NAME
red blend (see below)	2008
VARIETY	YEAR
Barossa Valley, South Australia	$15
ORIGIN	PRICE

CLOSURE

There really is a guy named Peter Lehmann; now eighty, he's been in the Aussie wine industry since he was a teenager. He's a legend, a guy who started a winery in the late '70s, at a time when there was a glut of grapes on the market and not much demand for wine. At least, not like there is today. He bailed out some grape-growing friends and became very successful. The rest, as the expression goes, is history.

This wild, beautiful blend of five varieties—Shiraz, Grenache, Mourvèdre, Tempranillo, and Carignan—is incredibly versatile when it comes to food pairing.

TRIVIA On the cap, you'll notice a black clubs symbol. The company's logo is the Queen of Clubs, apparently the card for gamblers; it symbolizes Peter Lehmann's gamble with his career and cash—not to mention the gamble of his investors.

PAIR WITH Spicy lamb, cassoulet, steak, stew, tagine, tomato-based pasta dishes, roast chicken.

UNCORK At big family gatherings, poker nights.

ST HALLETT

St Hallett	Faith
WINERY	WINE NAME
Shiraz	2008
VARIETY	YEAR
Barossa Valley, Australia	$22
ORIGIN	PRICE
	CLOSURE

Here's a wine for anyone who needs faith, whether it's believing in something, someone, or simply in the power of a good, rich, big red wine. The winery is named after a long-ago Aussie surveyor. As for the "saint" part of his name? No one knows.

TRIVIA We know Shiraz as wine (and a grape). "Hafez of Shiraz" was the name of a Sufi poet in the 1300s who wrote about love, faith, and drinking too much wine.

PAIR WITH Sausage, steak. Or drink by itself.

UNCORK For family get-togethers, any time someone says, "Bring a red," but doesn't tell you what they're making. Or cellar for a year or two.

TIC TOK

Robert Oatley Vineyards	James Oatley Tic Tok	
WINERY	WINE NAME	
Cabernet Sauvignon	2008	$16
VARIETY	YEAR	PRICE
New South Wales and Western Australia		
ORIGIN		CLOSURE

James Oatley is dead. Long live James Oatley—well, the wines named after him, anyway. Oatley was a British convict, banished to Australia. But he turned his life around in Oz and became one of the country's top clockmakers. This wine, created by his great-great-grandson, Bob Oatley, is a tribute to him. Get it? Tic Tok.

TRIVIA Bob Oatley is the man who created Rosemount wines in the late 1960s; he sold the winery in 2001, but not before it had become the second-most-popular Australian wine in the U.S. Robert Oatley Vineyards is his new label.

PAIR WITH Lamb, hard aged cheddar, steak, hamburgers, bison burgers.

UNCORK For hump day (time's a-tickin'), NHL playoffs (open at overtime!), Aussie fan club nights, when someone tells you to just "Bring a red."

THE WISHING TREE

The Australian Premium Wine Collection
....
WINERY

The Wishing Tree   Shiraz   2006
....
WINE NAME   VARIETY   YEAR

Western Australia $17
....
ORIGIN   PRICE   CLOSURE

The Australian Premium Wine Collection is a group of wineries hand-picked by an Aussie importer (with a top-notch palate) named John Larchet. Big, spicy, and powerful Shiraz wines from Oz are some of the most popular wines in Canada. You may know the big names, those massive wineries that made Shiraz a household name here, but why not try an excellent example from a smaller producer?

TRIVIA The winery's proprietor, John Larchet, says the Wishing Tree was an oak tree from his childhood in Ireland; when he was small, his parents told him that if he and his siblings made a wish under the tree, it would come true. Was that wish to drink great wine one day?

PAIR WITH Tagine, steak, lamb, venison, shawarma.

UNCORK Now, with dreamers, Yellow Tail drinkers, Aussie wine fan club members.

UNCORKED!

WYNNS COONAWARRA ESTATE

Wynns Coonawarra Estate	Black Label
WINERY	WINE NAME
Cabernet Sauvignon	2006
VARIETY	YEAR
Coonawarra, South Australia	$25
ORIGIN	PRICE

CLOSURE

Anyone who's had much in the way of Aussie red wines has probably had something from Coonawarra, maybe even a bottle of this classic Cabernet Sauvignon. The folks at Wynns (the oldest winery in the region) have been making it for fifty years, and they've mastered the formula. Ever hear someone say a red wine smells like chocolate or coffee, but you have no idea what they mean? Take a whiff of this bold beauty, and you'll understand.

TRIVIA The picture on the label is the famous Wynns three-gabled winery, which was built in 1896 by one John Riddoch, a Scottish pioneer who established the farm in 1860 and became stinkin' rich.

PAIR WITH Steak, steak, steak. Or sip by itself.

UNCORK At family gatherings, barbecues.

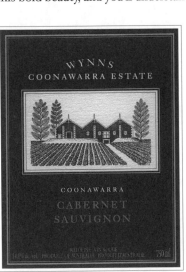

25/5

Bodegas del Desierto	25/5
WINERY	WINE NAME
Cabernet Sauvignon	2006
VARIETY	YEAR
La Pampa, Argentina	$25
ORIGIN	PRICE	CLOSURE

La Pampa is a new wine region in Argentina, but if this wine is any indication of quality, we'll be seeing a lot more from the region soon. This big, dark red wine has lots of great berry and smoky, spicy flavour; good tannins means it'll cellar if you want to stick a bottle or two away for a couple of years, until the region's really famous and you can whip out your back vintages and smugly say, "Ha! I knew about these guys *waaay* back when."

TRIVIA This wine gets its name from a date, May 25, which marks the anniversary of the institution of Argentina's first government independent from Spain. And "25 de Mayo" is also the name of a small town in the region where the wine is made.

PAIR WITH Steak or other barbecue dishes.

UNCORK On May 25, and at casual Friday get-togethers. Or stick in the cellar for a couple of years.

UNCORKED!

BARRANDICA

Antucura	Barrandica Estate Wine Selection	
WINERY	WINE NAME	
Cabernet Sauvignon/Merlot/Malbec		2008
VARIETIES		YEAR
Mendoza, Argentina	$25	
ORIGIN	PRICE	CLOSURE

Here's a big, smooth, rich, complex red that smells like a new leather jacket. That's a good thing. Really, this Bordeaux blend (aka Meritage, a fancy word that means it's a blend of Cabernet Sauvignon, Merlot, and Malbec) is just gorgeous, and a real consideration for your cellar if you're looking at building up a stash of bottles to try down the road. Tastes much more expensive than what it is.

TRIVIA The name Barrandica was inspired by the road that leads to the Antucura property, which, in addition to the world-class wines, features a seven-thousand-book library for guests to peruse. Just in case you're in the 'hood.

PAIR WITH Grilled lamb, steak, bison burgers, venison.

UNCORK For dinner with the boss, the first time you meet her parents, after a bad day at work. Or stick in the cellar for a couple of years.

BARRANDICA
ESTATE WINE
SELECTION
MENDOZA
ARGENTINA

CRIOS

Susana Balbo	Crios
WINERY	WINE NAME
Syrah-Bonarda	2008
VARIETIES	YEAR
Mendoza, Argentina	$20
ORIGIN	PRICE

CLOSURE

In a country and in an industry that are dominated primarily by male winemakers, Susana

Balbo has been making waves for more than twenty years; she considers the Crios line to be offspring (the secondary wines) to her parent line of wines, called Balbo. This red blend is young, fresh, and meant to be drunk now. And it's unfiltered; stand it upright for a day or so before serving so the sediment can settle down. And don't drain the bottle. Not quite, anyway.

TRIVIA Bonarda was, until recently, the most widely planted grape in Argentina. It goes by a few other names, too, including Corbeau, Douce Noir, and Charbonneau. A rose is a rose, by any other name.

PAIR WITH Steak, hamburgers, pizza, pot roast, prime rib.

UNCORK Now, at Mother's Day celebrations, family get-togethers, casual Friday celebrations.

DEL FIN DEL MUNDO

Bodega del Fin del Mundo
....
WINERY

Pinot Noir   2007
....
VARIETY   YEAR

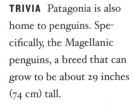

Patagonia, Argentina $20
....
ORIGIN   PRICE   CLOSURE

The winds are so crazy at the end of the world ("fin del mundo") that there are windbreak screens around the vineyards, and protective casings around each vine. And did I mention it's a desert? Despite special treatment and irrigation, you have to be tough to be a vine here. Tough is good, at least when it comes to making fine wine. Since its start in 2002, the winery has won more than 140 awards around the world. You'll want to give it an award, too.

TRIVIA Patagonia is also home to penguins. Specifically, the Magellanic penguins, a breed that can grow to be about 29 inches (74 cm) tall.

PAIR WITH Lamb, steak, salmon. Not penguin.

UNCORK At Grey Cup parties, barbecues, NHL playoffs, dinner with the boss.

DOÑA PAULA

Doña Paula	Los Cardos	
WINERY	WINE NAME	
Malbec	2008	
VARIETY	YEAR	
Mendoza, Argentina	$12	
ORIGIN	PRICE	CLOSURE

What Shiraz was to the 1990s, Malbec is fast becoming for the current decade. Malbec wines are big, lush, and really accessible—especially ones like Doña Paula's Los Cardos. The winery makes several different Malbecs, but the Los Cardos is especially affordable, easy to find, and a real crowd-pleaser.

Although Doña Paula is in Argentina, it has all kinds of international influences; it was started in 1997 by a group from Chile, and its winemakers boast Italian, German, French, and Spanish roots.

TRIVIA *Los cardos* are bright-coloured thistles: beautiful but a little dangerous. Their presence in a vineyard, however, is apparently a sign that the terroir (the dirt, vines, weather, etc.) is fantastic for growing grapes.

PAIR WITH Steak, Italian sausage. Or drink by itself.

UNCORK For tailgate parties, family gatherings, NHL playoffs, first dates, any time someone says, "Bring a red."

UNCORKED!

DON DAVID

Michel Torino Estate	Don David
WINERY	WINE NAME
Malbec	2009
VARIETY	YEAR
Cafayate Valley, Argentina	$19
ORIGIN	PRICE	CLOSURE

This winery was one of the first in Argentina to win an international award. That was in 1946, and some of the vines that still grow grapes for Michel Torino wines date back to that time. That's a good thing; older grapes make concentrated juice, which makes good vino. So drink up and enjoy this ballsy, smoky, spicy red. Don't be shy. The wine definitely isn't.

TRIVIA Don David is named after the winery's founder, David Michel; Don means "Mr." in Spanish.

PAIR WITH Steak, bison, meatballs, lamb.

UNCORK At dinners with Shiraz fans, family gatherings. Or stick in the cellar for a year or two.

FINCA LOS PRIMOS

Valentín Bianchi	Finca Los Primos
WINERY	WINE NAME
Malbec	2009
VARIETY	YEAR
Mendoza, Argentina	$14
ORIGIN	PRICE

CLOSURE

Sometimes you just want a red wine that's easy to find, that will go with lots of hearty meat dishes, and one you just enjoy by itself.

Here's that wine, a real crowd-pleaser. Valentín Bianchi is an Italian who moved to Argentina and started a winery. The name "San Rafael" on the label refers to a city in Mendoza, the heart of Argentina's wine country.

TRIVIA In South America, a *finca* is a ranch, a large chunk of rural property.

PAIR WITH Steak, lamb, burgers, ribs. Or drink by itself.

UNCORK Now, at dinner with the in-laws, when you have to bring a red wine but no one told you what's on the menu. Or cellar for up to five years.

PUNTO FINAL

Bodegas Renacer	Punto Final	
WINERY	WINE NAME	
Malbec	2009	
VARIETY	YEAR	
Mendoza, Argentina	$14	
ORIGIN	PRICE	CLOSURE

This wine is an outstanding example of the grape that's making Argentina's wines so famous around the world. What you can expect: a big, spicy, smoooooth (yeah, *that* smooth) red.

Punto Final isn't filtered, so don't jiggle it before opening; if it gets bumped around, let it stand for a day or two before opening it so that the sediment has time to sink to the bottom of the bottle again. And, if possible, decant.

TRIVIA Although the winery was only started in 2004, the vines that grow the grapes for this wine are all at least fifty years old.

PAIR WITH Steak, grilled red meat.

UNCORK Now, at dinner with wine geeks, dinner with the boss, the first time you meet his/her parents.

CHONO

Chono
....
WINERY

Cabernet Sauvignon   2007
....
VARIETY   YEAR

Maipo Valley, Chile $19
....
ORIGIN   PRICE   CLOSURE

This winery is named for the Chono, a native tribe that thrived, for a time, in the incredibly harsh environment of southern Chile. They were tough, but by the late 1800s, they were dead. All that is left is a handful of memories recorded by sailors who crossed paths with them. You'll have good memories when you drink this robust red that smells (and tastes) like berries and chocolate and pepper.

TRIVIA Winemaker Alvaro Espinoza worked at both Château Margaux, one of the top estates in Bordeaux, and the French champagne house Moët & Chandon.

PAIR WITH Medium-rare steak, steak, and—did I mention?—steak.

UNCORK For backyard barbecues, camping trips, dinners with the boss, family gatherings. Or stick in the cellar for a year or two.

UNCORKED!

CHONO
RESERVA

Cabernet Sauvignon
Maipo Valley · 2007
13.5% alc/vol.   750 mL
Wine · Product of Chile / Vin · Produit du Chili

CONCHA Y TORO

Concha y Toro	Trio Reserva
WINERY	WINE NAME

Cabernet Sauvignon/Shiraz/Cabernet Franc	2008
VARIETIES	YEAR

Maipo Valley, Chile	$18	
ORIGIN	PRICE	CLOSURE

One of Chile's oldest, largest, and most famous producers, Concha y Toro launched this brand of blends in 2004. The red? A spicy-smooth blend of Cabernet Sauvignon, Shiraz, and Cabernet Franc, it is a big, smooth, elegant wine, but in a macho, masculine sort of way. It's a suit, not jeans and a sweater.

TRIVIA The Concha y Toro winery—the biggest winery in South America—was started in 1883 by a Chilean politician who brought the vines for the winery from France.

PAIR WITH Barbecue, carpaccio, pâté, cheese.

UNCORK For the first snowfall, NHL playoffs, family get-togethers, casual Friday celebrations.

SIBARIS

Undurraga	Sibaris	
WINERY	WINE NAME	
Carménère	2007	
VARIETY	YEAR	
Colchagua Valley, Chile	$15	
ORIGIN	PRICE	CLOSURE

Carménère is the Viggo Mortensen of the wine world—it too is an Old World wonder that's been transported to the New World (Viggo went from Denmark to Hollywood; the grape went from Bordeaux, France, to Chile). In their new habitats, they're not just flourishing, they're stars.

As for the Undurraga winery, it was started in the 19th century by an entrepreneur named Don (as in "Mr.") Francisco Undurraga, who brought grapes from France and Germany to plant in Chile.

TRIVIA The Undurraga winery has been shipping wines to North America since 1903. And we classify Chilean wines as coming from the New World!

PAIR WITH Cheeseburgers, hamburgers, bison burgers, steak, grilled chicken, grilled vegetables.

UNCORK For NHL playoffs, taking the boss to dinner, at dinners with the in-laws. Or cellar for a couple of years.

UNCORKED!

NOTES

AND NOW, THE WHITE WINES

BLASTED CHURCH

Blasted Church	Hatfield's Fuse
WINERY	WINE NAME
white blend (see below)	2009
VARIETY	YEAR
Okanagan Valley, B.C.	$22
ORIGIN	PRICE

CLOSURE

If you're a wine snob, or one in training, maybe you'd dismiss this bottle because of the cartoonish label—eerie-looking people, including a stubble-cheeked guy with overalls and big bags under his eyes. But that's part of the charm of Blasted Church, one of those wineries where the people don't take themselves too seriously but still produce some seriously good wines.

Hatfield's Fuse is one of them, a white blend that smells like a spicy tropical fruit salad and is made from Gewürztraminer, Chardonnay, Ehrenfelser, Pinot Gris, Riesling, Sauvignon Blanc, and a relatively unknown grape called Optima. A mouthful? Yeah, but it works. Trust me.

TRIVIA In 1923 a group of guys from Okanagan Falls decided to move an old wooden church from a deserted mining camp. The plan? To "loosen the nails" with dynamite. (Hatfield was the last name of the guy who set off the fuses.) Their plan worked; the church now stands in Okanagan Falls, not far from the winery.

PAIR WITH Roast pork loin, Asian-style dishes such as tuna tataki, and Vietnamese sub sandwiches.

UNCORK While watching the fireworks at the Calgary Stampede, having dinner with the boss (show him/her you're a dynamite employee!). Serve chilled.

CEDARCREEK

CedarCreek Estate Winery	Proprietor's White
WINERY	WINE NAME
white blend (see below)	2008
VARIETY	YEAR
Okanagan Valley, B.C.	$14
ORIGIN	PRICE	CLOSURE

Here's a white wine for every white wine lover: a creative blend of Chardonnay, Pinot Gris, Pinot Blanc, Ehrenfelser, Gewürztraminer, and Riesling. CedarCreek's Proprietor's White is an entry-level wine, meaning it's an affordable way to find out if you like something from this winery before making a commitment to a bottle that may cost double the price or more.

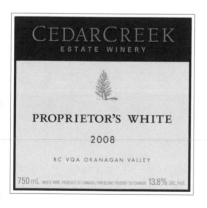

TRIVIA The proprietor at CedarCreek is Senator Ross Fitzpatrick (now retired). Born and raised in the Okanagan Valley, he went on to achieve fame and fortune in the rest of the province—but never forgot his valley roots. Now his son Gordon Fitzpatrick heads up the place, an imposing jewel of a winery.

PAIR WITH Roast chicken or turkey, niçoise salad, Indian takeout. Or serve by itself before dinner.

UNCORK For turkey day, when you're asked to bring a white wine but you don't know what's on the menu. Serve chilled.

UNCORKED!

QUAILS' GATE

Quails' Gate
....
WINERY

Chenin Blanc   2009
....
VARIETY   YEAR

Okanagan Valley, B.C. $19
....
ORIGIN   PRICE   CLOSURE

One of the Okanagan's oldest wineries, Quails' Gate has been making vino in the valley since 1956, and like so many big wineries in the region, this one remains owned and operated by the family that started it. As for the Chenin Blanc, it's one of those wines—citrusy, juicy, crispy, dry—that's so delicious it literally makes your mouth water.

TRIVIA U.S. President Barack Obama drank Quails' Gate Chenin Blanc when he was in Ottawa on his first official visit.

PAIR WITH Fresh oysters, linguini with clams, scallops, shrimp salad.

UNCORK Now, at Canada Day celebrations, patio parties. Serve chilled.

RED ROOSTER

Red Rooster		
WINERY		

Gewürztraminer	2009	
VARIETY	YEAR	

Okanagan Valley, B.C.	$16.50	
ORIGIN	PRICE	CLOSURE

Winemaker Karen Gillis thought she'd become a chef until she stumbled into her true calling: wine. She makes a lot of good wines, but the Gewürztraminer is especially fun and it smells good enough to eat, er, drink, uh, wear. Whatever. You know what I mean, and if you don't, you will once you try it. The name may sound like something you say to someone who's suffering from hay fever or a bad cold, but this Gewürztraminer is nothing to sneeze at.

TRIVIA If you're in the Okanagan, stop by the winery and ask to meet Frank the Baggage Handler. Don't be surprised when he's naked. That's all I'm saying.

PAIR WITH Sablefish, pad Thai, butter chicken, mild curry.

UNCORK Now, for patio parties, hot summer nights, Friday night takeout. Serve chilled.

SANDHILL

Sandhill		
WINERY		

Pinot Blanc	2007	
VARIETY	YEAR	

Okanagan Valley, B.C.	$22	
ORIGIN	PRICE	CLOSURE

Have to go to a dinner, and someone asked you to bring a Chardonnay? Try slipping this one past them instead. Right from the get-go, the folks at Sandhill—the uptown big sister to Calona Vineyards, British Columbia's first winery—have made wines that will make you want to sit up and take notice. Well, we're noticing. By the way, they make a Chardonnay, too, just in case you want to play by the rules.

TRIVIA Chief winemaker Howard Soon (king of the Sandhill?) started his career making beer before discovering his true passion, making award-winning wines.

PAIR WITH Roast chicken or turkey, smoked salmon, creamy pasta dishes, wild rice.

UNCORK Now, for patio parties, hot summer nights, Canada Day, turkey day. Serve chilled.

CAVE SPRING

Cave Spring
....
WINERY

Riesling (estate bottled)   2007
....
VARIETY   YEAR

Beamsville Bench, Niagara,
Ontario $22
....
ORIGIN   PRICE   CLOSURE

The folks at Cave Spring make eight Rieslings, including an icewine. I guess they know a thing or two about one of the most universally loved white wine grapes. This one—with the bird on the label—is very European in style: in other words, it smells like gasoline and wet rocks, but in a good way. (Wine geeks and geologists call that rock smell "minerality.") Lucky for non–rock groupies, it's also delicate and dry. A very versatile food wine.

TRIVIA The winery is co-owned by the owners of St. Urbans-Hof winery, one of Germany's most famous wineries and one that's also big on Riesling. Go figure.

PAIR WITH Turkey, roast chicken, ham, Thai green curries, Indian dishes, Italian salami, charcuterie.

UNCORK For turkey day, Easter, Canada Day, dinner with wine geeks. Serve chilled.

Estate Bottled

CAVE SPRING
2007
RIESLING
VQA BEAMSVILLE BENCH VQA
CAVE SPRING VINEYARD
CAVE SPRING CELLARS, JORDAN, ONTARIO, CANADA

SIBLING RIVALRY

Henry of Pelham	Sibling Rivalry	
WINERY	WINE NAME	
Riesling/Chardonnay/Gewürztraminer		2008
VARIETIES		YEAR
Niagara Peninsula, Ontario	$18	
ORIGIN	PRICE	CLOSURE

What happens when three brothers work together? Sometimes they fight. Doesn't matter how much they love each other. When Paul, Daniel, and Matthew Speck—owners of Henry of Pelham, one of Niagara's top wineries—scrap, they find creative ways to work out their issues. One way? Making wine. This crisp, super-fragrant white wine is made from a combination of Riesling, Chardonnay, and Gewürztraminer grapes—a variety for each brother. Don't miss the top of the screw cap, which features three sets of hands playing Rock, Paper, Scissors.

TRIVIA The Specks' great-great-great-grandfather Nicholas Smith farmed on the winery's land in 1794; his youngest son built the building that is now the wine story. His name? Henry. And the winery's address? Pelham Road.

PAIR WITH Shrimp masala, green Thai and coconut milk curries, pad Thai, Vietnamese subs. Or drink by itself.

UNCORK Now, with your siblings (if they have a sense of humour), for sunny patio days, mid-week (aka hump day), takeout. Chill well.

WILDASS

Stratus	Wildass	
WINERY	WINE NAME	
Riesling	2008	
VARIETY	YEAR	
Niagara Peninsula, Ontario	$18.50	
ORIGIN	PRICE	CLOSURE

Don't let the moniker fool you. You may not feel comfortable serving this wine to Mom, who might threaten to wash out your mouth with soap. (You can shout, "But Ma, I'm not swearing, honest!")

Pour her a glass. Show her the wee donkey on the label. Maybe you'll convince her. Maybe not. If she doesn't want it, well, that just means there's more for you. Or your friends—because you're going to want to throw a Wildass party after you try this semi-dry sipper.

TRIVIA Wildass wines (there are a few) are made by Stratus, one of Canada's top wineries.

PAIR WITH Indian curries, sushi, Vietnamese subs.

UNCORK Now, at stags, stagettes, patio parties, Stampede parties, hump day (Wildass Wednesday, anyone?), any time you need an excuse to cut loose and drink something good. Serve chilled.

UNCORKED!

THE ART OF WINE

The Art of Wine (Bluebird Wines)
....
WINERY

Chardonnay	$19	2008
VARIETY	PRICE	YEAR

California (wines are labelled in Alberta)

....
ORIGIN   CLOSURE

Calgarians Steve Wiggers and John Baker are young (in their twenties), and a while ago, they decided to start a winery, Bluebird Wines. They are now "licensed producers of wine in California." In other words, they hire a consulting winemaker, and they rent space in a winery in California. Then they buy grapes and create a few blends that they sell in Alberta under the "Art of Wine" moniker. Each label features an original artwork, too—their way of supporting the local arts community.

TRIVIA They are not artists; nor are they birdwatchers. The name "Bluebird" comes from a slang term for a great snowboarding day.

PAIR WITH Salmon, crab cakes.

UNCORK During casual Friday night get-togethers. Serve chilled.

FETZER

Fetzer Vineyards	Valley Oaks
WINERY	WINE NAME
Gewürztraminer	2008
VARIETY	YEAR
Mendocino, California	$15
ORIGIN	PRICE

CLOSURE

Now one of California's best-known wineries, Fetzer Vineyards was started in 1968, and ten years later became one of North America's first wineries to grow Gewürztraminer. ("Guh-VYRTS-trah-mee-nuhr," if you're struggling to get your tongue around those syllables.)

Although the wines aren't organic, winery staff and owners do show dedication to the environment; at the winery, they compost, recycle, and support various wildlife protection charities.

TRIVIA Since 1992, Fetzer has been owned by the Brown-Forman Corporation, the same company that owns Finlandia Vodka, Jack Daniel's, and Southern Comfort.

PAIR WITH Sushi, mild Indian curry, Vietnamese subs, Chinese food.

UNCORK For Friday night takeout, book clubs, bridal showers, patio parties, hot summer nights. Chill well.

UNCORKED!

LIBERTY SCHOOL

Liberty School
....
WINERY

Chardonnay   2007
....
VARIETY   YEAR

Central Coast, California $23
....
ORIGIN   PRICE   CLOSURE

AND NOW, THE WHITE WINES

When it comes to California, Chardonnay is the white wine that comes to mind for most of us when we think of the southern state. This Chardonnay is a fine example of the famous wine, from a family-owned winery (which can be rather rare). It has that creamy sort of taste that you'd expect from a California Chardonnay, but it's not over the top. You won't be tired of this one after a few sips. That can be good news or bad. Up to you to decide.

TRIVIA The Hope family, who own Liberty School, grew grapes for ten years for Caymus, one of California's most famous wineries; now they use those grapes for their own wines.

PAIR WITH Pork loin, veal, tortellini in cream sauce, roast chicken or turkey.

UNCORK For family get-togethers, high school reunions, turkey day. Chill well.

MIRTH

Corvidae Wine Company	Mirth	
WINERY	WINE NAME	
Chardonnay	2009	
VARIETY	YEAR	
Columbia Valley, Washington	$20	
ORIGIN	PRICE	CLOSURE

The average five year old laughs about four hundred times a day. The average adult? About fifteen. Hmm . . . We grownups could obviously use some Mirth in our lives.

This Chardonnay, from an Irish-American winemaker named David O'Reilly, is unoaked, meaning it doesn't have that buttery, almost thick flavour that some Chards do.

So if you're part of the ABC (anything but Chardonnay) camp, ignore your expectations and give this one a try. You'll be pleasantly surprised, and after a glass or two, you may even laugh.

TRIVIA The word *corvidae* refers to the scientific classification for the family of birds that includes crows, blue jays, and ravens. As for "Mirth"? From an ancient nursery rhyme about magpies.

PAIR WITH Turkey, chicken (of course!), mussels, prawns, sablefish.

UNCORK On the first day of spring, the last day of summer, when you have something to crow about. Chill well.

UNCORKED!

mirth
2009 CHARDONNAY

ATTITUDE

Pascal Jolivet	Attitude	
WINERY	WINE NAME	
Sauvignon Blanc	2008	
VARIETY	YEAR	
Loire Valley, France	$23	
ORIGIN	PRICE	CLOSURE

This fresh, fun wine is a great introduction to one of France's most interesting winemakers, whose family—like that of so many European winemakers—has been cranking out *les vins* for many generations. (His last name, by the way, is pronounced "ZHO-lee-vay," for anyone who doesn't speak even a little French.)

Attitude comes from a region that specializes in Sauvignon Blanc. The name says it all; you're allowed to have attitude when you're this good.

TRIVIA The Romans planted the first vineyards in the Loire Valley two thousand years ago; Jolivet started his winery in 1987.

PAIR WITH Shrimp salad, sushi, fresh raw oysters, crab, sole or other white fish.

UNCORK Now, at dinner with wine geeks, dinner with Francophiles, patio parties. Chill well.

DOMAINE DE VAUFUGET

Domaine de Vaufuget
....
WINERY

Chenin Blanc   2008
....
VARIETY   YEAR

Vouvray, Loire Valley, France $20.25
....
ORIGIN   PRICE   CLOSURE

French wines—at least, those from the most famous regions, like Burgundy, Bordeaux, and the Loire Valley—are often good, but they aren't often fun. They're serious wines for serious wine drinkers. With that in mind, this label isn't going to convince you that you'll have a good time if you drink it. But trust me; it's fun, a little crisp, a little sweet, a little floral. Still not convinced? It's flexible, food friendly, and it's going to hold a party, whether you show up or not.

TRIVIA The word *Vouvray* simply refers to part of the Loire Valley, where Chenin Blanc is the most popular wine grape. (Vouvray is 100 percent Chenin Blanc.)

PAIR WITH Spicy noodle dishes, scallops and shrimp, goat cheese dishes, cheese fondues.

UNCORK Now, when dining with Francophiles, impressing a wine geek, drinking with the ABC (anything but Chardonnay) white wine club. Serve chilled.

UNCORKED!

GENTIL "HUGEL"

Hugel et Fils	Gentil "Hugel"	
WINERY	WINE NAME	
white blend (see below)	2009	
VARIETY	YEAR	
Alsace, France	$17	
ORIGIN	PRICE	CLOSURE

Here's a creative, lemony fresh blend of wine from Gewürztraminer, Pinot Gris, Riesling, Muscat, and Sylvaner grapes. Tell someone in English that their wine is "nice," and it might sound like an insult, like you are too afraid to tell them how you really feel. Say it in French—*gentil*—and suddenly it sounds a whole lot sexier. That's this wine. Creative. Suave. Very, very European, and very food friendly, too. And that's no lie.

TRIVIA The Hugel family has been making wine in France's Alsace region since the 1600s.

PAIR WITH Sushi, curry, Chinese food, white fish.

UNCORK For hump day, Friday night takeout. Serve chilled.

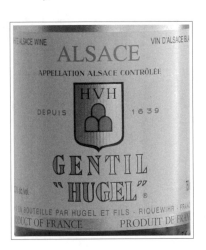

LE JAJA DE JAU

Château de Jau	Le Jaja de Jau	
WINERY	WINE NAME	
Sauvignon Blanc	2008	
VARIETY	YEAR	
Côtes de Gascogne, France	$16	
ORIGIN	PRICE	CLOSURE

I'm a sucker for a fun label, and this loopy, handwritten black-and-white number gets me every time. Apparently it's by an artist named Ben Vauthier who has been friends with the winery owners for several years. "Le Jaja" refers to wine for everyday drinking, wine for pleasure, for thirst. I'll drink to that. I'll drink this wine, in fact; it's fresh and crisp and mouth-watering. Think lemons and limes and the smell of wet earth after a spring rain.

TRIVIA In Catalan, the word *jaja* refers to a glass of wine—any colour—paired with a small plate of food (maybe some cured meat, or some cheese and a chunk of bread).

PAIR WITH Tapas-style appetizers and salads. Or drink by itself.

UNCORK Now, for patio parties, Friday nights, any time you want to pretend you're in France. Serve chilled.

UNCORKED!

PIERRE SPARR

Pierre Sparr
....
WINERY

Pinot Gris   2007
....
VARIETY   YEAR

Alsace, France $23
....
ORIGIN   PRICE   CLOSURE

Don't expect this Pinot Gris to taste like any Pinot Grigios you may have had from Italy. Yes, it's the same grape, but the style's a bit different: this one's bigger, fuller, more lush. But it's just as food friendly and yummy.

Nine generations of Sparrs have been making wine at this estate, which was established in 1680; Pierre Sparr rebuilt the property after it was destroyed during the Second World War.

TRIVIA The French word *pinot* means "pine cone," and here refers to the shape of the grape clusters on the vine.

PAIR WITH Grilled white fish or salmon, Thai green curries, roast chicken, roasted Mediterranean vegetables, ham, pork loin. Serve chilled.

UNCORK For turkey day, Easter dinner, when you need to impress your Francophile friends. Chill well.

SIRIUS

Sirius		
WINERY		
mostly Sauvignon Blanc	2009	
VARIETY	YEAR	
Bordeaux, France	$23	
ORIGIN	PRICE	CLOSURE

Are you Sirius? Maybe not, but this wine is—an elegant, young but Old World beauty of a white wine; if Audrey Tautou or Marion Cotillard were wines, this is what they'd be. Primarily Sauvignon Blanc, this wine has a bit of Muscadelle thrown into its blend to make it smell pretty (less citrus and more floral aromatics). Check out the red Bordeaux blend, too, an outstanding mix of Merlot and Cabernet Sauvignon.

Sirius is the brainchild of one of France's best-known wine families, the Sichel family, who own Chateau Palmer, one of the most famous labels in Bordeaux.

TRIVIA Also known as the "Dog Star," Sirius is the brightest star in our sky. Polynesians once used it to navigate around the Pacific Ocean. Use the wine to help navigate yourself through the sometimes-intimidating French section of wine shops.

PAIR WITH Roast chicken, mussels, salads.

UNCORK During the dog days of summer, wedding showers, baby showers, Francophile gatherings, book club meetings, dinner with wine snobs. Serve chilled.

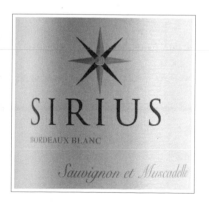

DR. L

Loosen Bros.	Dr. L	
WINERY	WINE NAME	
Riesling	2008	
VARIETY	YEAR	
Mosel, Germany	$17	
ORIGIN	PRICE	CLOSURE

An apple a day keeps the doctor away? Skip the apples, then, because this is one doctor you'll want in your fridge. Pronounced "LOH-zen," this winery has been family-owned (yeah, by the Loosens) for more than two hundred years. They started making this wine several years ago, and it's been a big hit, both in Germany and internationally, ever since. Sweet but not too sweet, with an ever-so-slight hint of effervescence, this wine tastes like a perfect summer day in a bottle.

TRIVIA Winemaker Ernst Loosen trained as an archae-ologist before taking over the family business.

PAIR WITH Spicy Thai cuisine, Indian curries, hot wings, pretty much anything with chili and a kick. Or just enjoy by itself.

UNCORK Now, for casual Fri-day gatherings, January days (those ones when you need a mental break from winter), tailgate parties, patio parties. Chill well.

LINGENFELDER

Lingenfelder	Bird Label
WINERY	**WINE NAME**
Riesling	2007
VARIETY	**YEAR**
Pfaltz, Germany	$15
ORIGIN	**PRICE**	**CLOSURE**

I just love the cute little bird and the pretty tree on the label—but best of all, the wine is as good as the label. (Alas, that's not always the case.) The Vineyard Creatures line of wines from Lingenfelder all feature, well, a vineyard creature: owl, hare, fish, fox, and bee. They're all worth seeking out. But one of the easiest to find? The Bird Label Riesling. It's remarkably approachable, without the impossible-to-pronounce Teutonic labels that so many German Rieslings have. Easy. Friendly. Delicious.

TRIVIA Go online to lingenfelder.com to find a tasting mat, a printable placemat of Lingenfelder wines, so you can host a vineyard-critter wine-tasting party. Cool.

PAIR WITH Indian everything, Thai green curries, Vietnamese subs, spicy noodle bowls.

UNCORK For hump day, patio parties, Asian takeout. Chill well.

URBAN

St. Urbans-Hof	Urban (Nik Weis Selection)
WINERY	WINE NAME
Riesling	2008
VARIETY	YEAR
Mosel, Germany	$15.50
ORIGIN	PRICE · CLOSURE

You can't get any more modern than a wine named *Urban*. But don't be fooled. This crisp Riesling has deep, ancient roots: a family-owned winery, St. Urbans-Hof, in Germany's dreamy Mosel River Valley. Nik Weis—a man with a rock-star moniker—is the winemaker here.

TRIVIA Lots. First, St. Urban is the patron saint of wine-making, and *hof* just means "estate." Secondly, Hermann Weis, son of the winery's founder, planted Niagara's first large plot of Riesling vines in the early 1970s; that land eventually became Vineland Estates Winery.

PAIR WITH Sushi, Indian takeout, pad Thai, spicy chicken wings.

UNCORK For dinner with wine geeks, Friday night takeout. Chill well.

RABL

Weingut Rudolf Rabl
....
WINERY

Grüner Veltliner   2008
....
VARIETY   YEAR

Spiegel (vineyard), Kamptal,
Austria $19
....
ORIGIN   PRICE   CLOSURE

The Rabl family, who own this winery, have been farming on this estate since 1750; in fact, their cellar was built at least three hundred years ago. And like the Rabl family, Grüner Veltliner wines go back a long, long way in Austrian history; they're considered to be the nation's signature white wine. Throughout the years, winemakers have tweaked their formulas to keep up with the times. This modern, very dry white wine is a fine example.

TRIVIA The town of Langenlois, in Austria's Kamptal region, is home to the Loisium, a museum all about the country's wines. And *weingut* is the German word for winery.

PAIR WITH Ham and other cured meats, Chinese food, Asian fusion dishes, crab cakes, asparagus, artichokes, pork roasts with applesauce.

UNCORK For Easter, book club, hump day takeout. Serve chilled.

UNCORKED!

WEINGUT JURTSCHITSCH

Weingut Jurtschitsch	GrüVe
WINERY	WINE NAME
Grüner Veltliner	2007
VARIETY	YEAR
Kamptal, Austria	$24
ORIGIN	PRICE

CLOSURE

Cork dorks call Grüner Veltliner (pronounced "GROO-nuhr VELT-lee-nuhr") the "groovy" grape, hence the name of this fun wine. Although Grüner Veltliner is grown in other parts of the world, it originated in Austria and has become one of the country's signature grapes. Big surprise—that's where this wine comes from. What to expect when you open it? A spicy fruit bomb that will kick-start your taste buds. Very, very food friendly, too.

TRIVIA The label is a reproduction of a painting by a famous Austrian artist named Christian Ludwig Attersee; every year, he paints a different one, just for the GrüVe. The 2007 art is entitled *GrüVe Dance*, which is what you'll be doing if you drink too much of it.

PAIR WITH Sushi, mild Indian curry, Vietnamese subs, Chinese food.

UNCORK During book clubs, Friday night takeout, stagettes, patio parties, hot summer nights. Serve chilled.

GABBIANO

Castello di Gabbiano
....
WINERY

Pinot Grigio   2008
....
VARIETY   YEAR

Italy $11.50
....
ORIGIN   PRICE   CLOSURE

The actual Gabbiano estate (and winery) is in Tuscany, about a twenty-minute drive from Florence. But this wine is made from grapes grown closer to Venice, hence the words *delle Venezie* on the label. This simple white sipper is citrusy, fresh, and not too acidic; a typical Italian summer wine, it is best when served with food.

Pinot Grigio, also known as Pinot Gris, is a wacky grape that's prone to mutation. Depending where they're planted (they grow all over the world), the grapes can be bluish- or brownish-pink. The one thing the mutants have in common? They produce wines that aren't very aromatic, so if you can't smell a lot when you're drinking a Pinot Grigio, you're not alone.

TRIVIA The image of the knight on the Gabbiano label is a reproduction of one found on the remains of an ancient fresco at the estate.

PAIR WITH Italian cured meats and cheeses, grilled white fish or chicken, pasta salads.

UNCORK Now, at patio parties. Serve chilled.

LUZANO

Marotti Campi	Luzano
WINERY	WINE NAME
Verdicchio del Castelli di Jesi	2008
VARIETY (AND APPELLATION)	YEAR
Marche, Italy	$23
ORIGIN	PRICE

CLOSURE

Yes, that's a very long and rather complicated name. Call it Luzano, if you're trying to remember it. As for the grape? It's Verdicchio, a popular white grape in Italy's Marche region; the name refers to the colour *verde* ("green" in Italian). Elegant, unusual. One that will likely please every white-wine fan.

TRIVIA Marotti Campi has been a family-owned estate for more than one hundred years. Now it's being called "a rising star." So's the region—it's not yet overrun with tourists.

PAIR WITH Paella, sablefish, halibut, chicken.

UNCORK Now, at casual family gatherings, dinner with wine geeks. Or stick in the cellar. This is one of the only indigenous Italian whites that ages well. Be sure to chill well.

INFINITUS

Cosecheros y Criadores	Infinitus	
WINERY	WINE NAME	
Gewürztraminer	2008	
VARIETY	YEAR	
Castilla, Spain	$15	
ORIGIN	PRICE	CLOSURE

Gewürztraminer wines tend to be a bit intimidating for new wine fans. Here's the first thing you need to know: it's pronounced "guh-VYRTS-trah-mee-nuhr." Not so scary now, right?

And the style of the Infinitus Gewürztraminer? This silky, fresh beauty is all roses and jasmine and spice—it's so yummy, you'll want to bottle it as a fragrance, not just drink it.

TRIVIA Central Spain—where this wine comes from—is apparently the world's largest wine-growing region, larger than Australia and Chile's regions combined.

PAIR WITH Sushi, mild Indian curry, Vietnamese subs, Chinese food.

UNCORK For book clubs, bridal showers, patio parties, hot summer nights, with Friday night takeout. Serve chilled.

PLÉYADES

Pléyades
WINERY

Macabeo   2009
VARIETY   YEAR

Cariñena, Spain $15
ORIGIN   PRICE   CLOSURE

AND NOW, THE WHITE WINES

Also known as Viura, Macabeo is one of Spain's most popular grapes and is one of the grapes used in cava, Spain's version of champagne. Here, Macabeo—pronounced "MAK-a-bayo"—has been turned into a crisp white still wine (as in no bubbles) that smells (and tastes) like grapefruit and lemons and nectarines. Nice.

TRIVIA In ancient Greek mythology, Pleione was a nymph from the ocean; she married Atlas, the god of heavy burdens, who held the heavens in his hands. Pleione gave birth to seven beautiful daughters, who were turned into doves and then stars: the Pleiades constellation. This wine is named in their honour.

PAIR WITH Salads, shrimp cocktail. Or drink by itself.

UNCORK Now, for patio nights, the last days of summer, romantic dinners. Serve chilled.

QUINTA DO AMEAL

Quinta do Ameal

WINERY

Loureiro   2008

VARIETY   YEAR

Lima, Portugal $17.50

ORIGIN   PRICE   CLOSURE

This wine is a Vinho Verde, which literally means "green wine" in Portuguese. That doesn't mean it's green coloured, however; it just means that it's young, and that's the way it's supposed to be. (Don't stick this one in the cellar.) Quinta do Ameal's wine is made from organic Loureiro grapes, a Portuguese variety that's popular for Vinho Verde. It smells a little like flowers and tastes a lot like lemons and grapefruit.

TRIVIA Pedro Araujo, whose family owns Quinta do Ameal, is the grandson of Adriano Ramos Pinto, founder of the legendary Ramos Pinto port house.

PAIR WITH Salad; Chinese, Thai, Vietnamese, and Indian takeout. Or add fresh peach slices and cranberry or pomegranate juice for a cool "wine-tail," aka a cocktail made with wine.

UNCORK Now, for patio parties, hot summer nights, with organic food lovers. Serve chilled.

UNCORKED!

KANENAS

Tsantali	Kanenas Odyssey Rhapsody	
WINERY	WINE NAME	

Muscat of Alexandria–Chardonnay		2009
VARIETIES		YEAR

Moronia in Thrace, Greece	$19	
ORIGIN	PRICE	CLOSURE

Wandering around a wine shop and looking for something new to try? You might be tempted to walk past this short, squat bottle, because it doesn't look like the other bottles on the shelf. But put a couple in your basket and get ready to smile. If you like fragrant whites (think good fruit and beautiful flowers) with lots of personality that don't cost a bomb, you'll like this wine.

TRIVIA According to a Greek myth, a Cyclops trapped Odysseus in a cave; to escape, Odysseus offered the monster wine. The one-eyed dude became so enchanted by the wine, Odysseus blinded him—and then made his getaway. As Odysseus ran away, the Cyclops asked him what his name was. "*Kanenas,*" Odysseus replied, which means "no one." This wine won't make you go blind or see monsters, but you will be enchanted.

PAIR WITH Cold seafood salad, white fish, pasta salad, calamari. Or drink by itself.

UNCORK For patio parties, dinners with wine geeks, Chill well.

DURBANVILLE HILLS

Durbanville Hills
WINERY

Sauvignon Blanc | 2008
VARIETY | YEAR

Durbanville, South Africa | $12
ORIGIN | PRICE | CLOSURE

Sometimes inexpensive white wines taste like chemicals. One sip, and you wonder why anyone would bother. Not the case with this crisp, refreshing Sauvignon Blanc, a fine example of the varietal, and a price that can't be beat. It has great acidity (your mouth will feel like it's watering after you taste it), and it's aromatic, too: grapefruit, lime, and maybe papaya. Fresh papaya, not one that's been sitting in your fridge too long.

While the wine technically isn't organic, the winery does practice social responsibility and high environmental standards. A percentage of sales from each bottle goes into a trust to improve the standard of living for employees and their children.

TRIVIA The area of Durbanville gets its name from a Brit named Sir Benjamin D'Urban. He wasn't one of the most politically correct men in history, but he became the governor of the Cape Colony (part of what we now call South Africa). He eventually ended up in Canada, where he was named commander of the Queen's Forces in British North America. He died in Montreal in 1849.

PAIR WITH Salads, white fish, goat-cheese tarts, tomato-based pastas.

UNCORK On the patio, hot summer days. Serve chilled.

MAP MAKER

Staete Landt	Map Maker	
WINERY	WINE NAME	
Sauvignon Blanc	2009	
VARIETY	YEAR	
Marlborough, New Zealand	$20	
ORIGIN	PRICE	CLOSURE

More than 350 years ago, a Dutch explorer named Abel Tasman landed in what is now New Zealand; he mapped the coastline and named it *Staete Landt*, meaning "the land of the governors." Maybe you don't know where New Zealand is on a map, but you should try to at least find the NZ section of your nearest wine shop. Then ask for this shiny, bright Sauvignon Blanc.

TRIVIA New Zealand's connection with the Netherlands continues with this winery, which is owned by a Dutch couple—Ruud Maasdam and Dorien Vermaas. This wine, Map Maker, pays tribute to Tasman and his accomplishments.

PAIR WITH Seared scallops, avocado-shrimp salads, goat-cheese tarts.

UNCORK For patio parties, dinner with the boss, meeting his/her parents for the first time. Serve chilled.

WIRRA WIRRA

Wirra Wirra	Scrubby Rise	
WINERY	WINE NAME	

Sauvignon Blanc/Sémillon/Viognier		2009
VARIETIES		YEAR

South Australia	$14	
ORIGIN	PRICE	CLOSURE

To make things a little easier, let's just call this "Scrubby Rise." Really, it will save trying to pronounce all those long and complicated grapes stuck at the end of the name. Those grapes, though, are what make this wine so refreshing and good smelling, all floral and fruity and delicious. ("Smells like gummies," I once heard a five-year-old say when he stuck his nose in his mom's glass for a whiff.)

TRIVIA *Wirra Wirra* is an Australian aboriginal name meaning "among the gum trees."

PAIR WITH Salads with light dressings, artichokes, asparagus, chicken.

UNCORK Now, at patio parties, picnics. Serve chilled.

UNCORKED!

WIRRA WIRRA

Scrubby Rise

SAUVIGNON BLANC
SEMILLON
VIOGNIER

PRODUCT OF AUSTRALIA / PRODUIT D'AUSTRALIE
WHITE WINE / VIN BLANC   750ml

CARINAE

CarinaE Viñedos & Bodega
WINERY

Torrontés
VARIETY

2009
YEAR

Mendoza, Argentina
ORIGIN

$19
PRICE

CLOSURE

A French couple named Brigitte and Philippe Subra moved to Argentina in 1998, and in 2003, they opened CarinaE Viñedos & Bodega. The rest, as the expression goes, is history. They teamed up with France's "flying winemaker" Michel Rolland, a guy who gets paid by winery owners around the world to make their wines famous.

Torrontés is Argentina's most famous white wine grape; it makes crisp, aromatic white wines, and Rolland says Torrontés will one day be as popular as Chardonnay. The guy knows a thing or two about wine. I, for one, am listening.

TRIVIA Carina is a constellation in the southern hemisphere, visible from the vineyards where the Torrontés grapes are grown. The word *CarinaE* means "of Carina."

PAIR WITH Sushi, mussels, prawns, clams, grilled white fish, grilled or roasted chicken, goat-cheese tarts, brie. Or as an aperitif by itself.

UNCORK For chick nights, book clubs, wedding showers. Serve chilled.

CLAVA

Viña Quintay	Clava
WINERY	WINE NAME
Sauvignon Blanc	2008
VARIETY	YEAR
Casablanca Valley, Chile	$15.50
ORIGIN	PRICE	CLOSURE

Go with the flow with this zesty white wine from a winery whose name, *Quintay*, literally means "setting sail with the current" in Mapudungun, one of the tribal languages of the region. As for winemaker Vicente Johnson, he's considered to be one of Chile's rising stars, a young (well, youngish) guy who's especially renowned for his Sauvignon Blancs.

TRIVIA Sauvignon Blanc was one of the world's first wines to be bottled with a screwcap closure.

PAIR WITH Tossed salads, sablefish, halibut, rice salads.

UNCORK Now, with wine geeks, for patio parties, hot summer nights, camping trips. Serve chilled.

UNCORKED!

CONO SUR

Cono Sur		
WINERY		

Viognier	2009	
VARIETY	YEAR	

Colchagua Valley, Chile	$12	
ORIGIN	PRICE	CLOSURE

Cono Sur has been around for ages, and the wines are all consistently good—and many are organic these days. So, why did I choose the Viognier? Why not, say, the Cabernet Sauvignon, or the Pinot Noir? Well, the Viognier is very pretty, and it's relatively unusual. Viognier (pronounced "vee-own-yay") is often used as a blend with other grapes—in other words, it's usually the bridesmaid, seldom the bride. But here, it gets to be the bride. The princess. And she shines, with pretty aromas of melon, spice, and apricot. Not organic, but definitely good.

TRIVIA The bicycle on the label stands for the winery's environmental commitment (it was the world's first carbon-neutral winery); vineyard workers travel among the vines by bicycle.

PAIR WITH Sushi, falafel, pasta salad, teriyaki chicken, seafood salad, Vietnamese subs, Thai green curry.

UNCORK For patio days, book clubs, hump day (aka Wednesday), casual Fridays with friends. Chill well.

COUSIÑO MACUL

Cousiño Macul	Antiguas Reservas	
WINERY	WINE NAME	
Chardonnay	2008	
VARIETY	YEAR	
Maipo Valley, Chile	$17	
ORIGIN	PRICE	CLOSURE

This family-owned winery is now in the hands of the sixth generation of Cousiños, and they've been making Chardonnay since 1969.

This creamy, fruity, buttery, medium-bodied Chardonnay is just the ticket for anyone who loves typical California Chardonnay, but wants to bust out and try something new. Or not.

TRIVIA The word *Macul* comes from the Quechua language, spoken by the indigenous people in the region. It means "right hand." As for the company logo, it may just look like a bunch of pretty curvy lines, but it's actually a fancy stack of the letters in the family's name, Cousiño.

PAIR WITH Grilled chicken, salads, sablefish, halibut.

UNCORK For hump day, casual Fridays with friends, lunching with the ladies, patio days. Chill well.

NOTES

RA! RA!
ROSÉ!
(PINK
DRINKS)

THE OJAI VINEYARD

The Ojai Vineyard
WINERY

rosé blend   2009
VARIETY   YEAR

Central Coast, California $25
ORIGIN   PRICE   CLOSURE

Despite the spelling, Ojai is pronounced "Oh, hi!" Such a friendly place, and a friendly wine, too. A lunch wine for "an unbearably hot day," says the winemaker at Ojai. The Ojai Vineyard is a cult favourite among wine fans, primarily for its Syrah (Old World, aka French-style) red wines. But they're pricey. This pretty slurper is not. Enjoy.

TRIVIA A lot of famous people have lived in and around the small town of Ojai (which means "valley of the moon," according to the region's indigenous people), including Jerry Bruckheimer, Johnny Depp, Reese Witherspoon, and Jake Gyllenhaal.

PAIR WITH Quiche, salad, smoked salmon.

UNCORK Now, with wine geeks or for patio parties. Maybe both. Serve chilled.

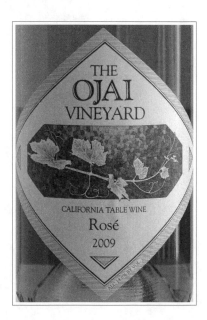

THE
OJAI
VINEYARD

CALIFORNIA TABLE WINE
Rosé
2009

MOULIN DE TOULOT

Moulin de Toulot		
WINERY		
rosé blend	2008	
VARIETY	YEAR	
Gascogne, France	$18	
ORIGIN	PRICE	CLOSURE

Gascogny, as we say in English, is mostly famous for its Armagnac, a distilled brandy made from grapes. But this crisp, light-tasting Old World rosé (it's almost orange, really) is worlds away from that. You can drink it any time, anywhere, with anyone. Don't think about it too much. Just chill it, open it, and enjoy it.

TRIVIA Real men drink rosé. French writer Alexandre Dumas modelled one of the Three Musketeers after a guy named Charles de Batz, who hailed from Gascony and loved good food and wine— the wine from Gascony.

PAIR WITH Chicken, Indian takeout, Vietnamese subs, smoked salmon, soft goat cheese.

UNCORK For bridal showers, turkey day, brunches, patio parties. Serve chilled.

OLLIEUX ROMANIS

Château Ollieux Romanis
WINERY

rosé blend   2008
VARIETY   YEAR

Corbières, France $17
ORIGIN   PRICE   CLOSURE

This wine hails from Corbières, in France's trendy Languedoc region. A pale salmon colour, it tastes dry, crisp, austere, and a bit mysterious. Think of it as the Catherine Deneuve of the wine world, versus, say, an Anna Nicole Smith kind of big, blowsy vino. They both have their charms, it's true. But although you may check out the big, blowsy wine, you'll want to be with the Château Ollieux for a long, long time.

TRIVIA Peer closely at the label and you'll see the winery's emblem: an olive tree coming out of a crown. The word *ollieux* refers to the handful of olive trees on the estate, some of which have been there for more than sixty years.

PAIR WITH Spicy Asian cuisine, Mediterranean-style tapas dishes, or serve by itself.

UNCORK Now, for dinners with Francophiles, third-date nights, impressing the wine geeks, or cellar up to two years. Serve chilled.

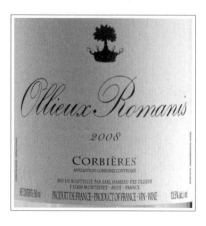

RÉSERVE DES VIGNERONS

Cave de Saumur	Réserve des Vignerons	
WINERY	WINE NAME	

Cabernet Franc	Cabernet de Saumur	2008
VARIETY	APPELLATION	YEAR

Loire Valley, France	$19	
ORIGIN	PRICE	CLOSURE

This is one of those perfect summer-day wines, when all you have to do is watch the clouds go by. Or, better yet, just lie in the grass and watch the blue sky. Yes, a pink wine—made from 100 percent Cabernet Franc—for a blue-sky day. There should be more of those. From Saumur, a region within France's famous Loire Valley, this easy-going sipper will make every day feel like summer.

TRIVIA Saumur is also famous for its religious-medal industry, its aluminum, and its mushrooms. (It's apparently the mushroom capital of France. Who knew?)

PAIR WITH Indian takeout, chicken, Vietnamese subs.

UNCORK For bridal showers, brunches, patio parties, hump day, casual Friday night gatherings. Serve chilled.

UNCORKED!

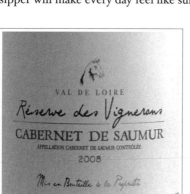

VAL DE LOIRE
Réserve des Vignerons
CABERNET DE SAUMUR
APPELLATION CABERNET DE SAUMUR CONTRÔLÉE
2008
Mis en Bouteille à la Propriété

TERRASSES

Château Pesquié	Terrasses
WINERY	WINE NAME
Cinsault/Grenache/Syrah	2008
VARIETIES	YEAR
Rhône Valley, France	$18
ORIGIN	PRICE

CLOSURE

Not for fans of sweet blush wines, this pretty, rose-hued sipper is definitely on the dry side. This blend of Cinsault, Grenache, and Syrah grapes is crisp, with fresh berry notes and good acidity—wine-geek talk for something fresh and tasty. Don't cellar this baby for long, though; it's made to drink now. And if you like the rosé, look for the lovely Terrasses red, a food-friendly blend of Grenache and Syrah.

TRIVIA Grapes have been grown on the Château Pesquié property for more than two thousand years. The word *pesquié* is Provençal slang for "fish pond." The third-generation winemakers who own the property now bought it from an heir to famous French novelist Alphonse Daudet.

PAIR WITH Fresh oysters, charcuterie, salads, soft cheeses (chèvre, for instance), simply prepared grilled fish.

UNCORK For hot afternoons on the patio, baby showers, dinner with wine snobs. Serve chilled.

Terrasses

VENTOUX – RHÔNE VALLEY VINEYARDS
2008

CHÂTEAU
PESQUIÉ

MARQUÉS DE CÁCERES

Marqués de Cáceres		
WINERY		
Tempranillo-Grenache	2008	
VARIETIES	YEAR	
Rioja, Spain	$13.50	
ORIGIN	PRICE	CLOSURE

Very intense and fruity, but with good acidity, it will help bridge the gap between red wine lovers and those who prefer white wine—and, for that matter, fans of berry coolers who are realizing there might be more to life than vodka, sugar, and artificial colours. A blend of Tempranillo and Grenache (Garnacha in Spain) grapes means it's very, very food friendly.

TRIVIA The winery was started in the 1960s by two French guys who owned a couple of hotshot French wineries; they then invited legendary consulting wine-maker Michel Rolland to help them out.

PAIR WITH Paella, pork, charcuterie with olives or even pickles, salmon, chicken, anything with ore-gano and thyme. Or drink as an aperitif.

UNCORK Now, on the patio, baby showers, camping trips, dinner with wine snobs on a super-tight budget. Serve chilled.

SANTA DIGNA

Miguel Torres	Santa Digna Reserve Rosé	
WINERY	WINE NAME	
Cabernet Sauvignon	2009	
VARIETY	YEAR	
Central Chile	$13.75	
ORIGIN	PRICE	CLOSURE

To quote from one of the *Sesame Street* songs I used to sing when I was little, "One of these things is not like the others." That would be this rosé, which is made from Cabernet Sauvignon grapes, generally used for big tannic reds. This rosiest of rosés certainly has that influence—it's almost as big and bold as a rosé can be.

The Torres family has been making wine in Spain for more than three hundred years, and while many of those wines—especially the reds—are legendary among wine fans, the New World wines from this family are also worth checking out.

TRIVIA This news isn't trivial at all: the Torres winery in Curicó, Chile—where this wine was made—was badly damaged, and thousands of bottles were destroyed, during the massive earthquake in early 2010. Organizations such as the Canadian Red Cross help people around the world during natural disasters; to make a donation, go to redcross.ca.

PAIR WITH Tomato-based pasta sauces, Chinese food, charcuterie meats. Or drink by itself.

UNCORK For Friday night dinner with friends, patio parties. Serve chilled.

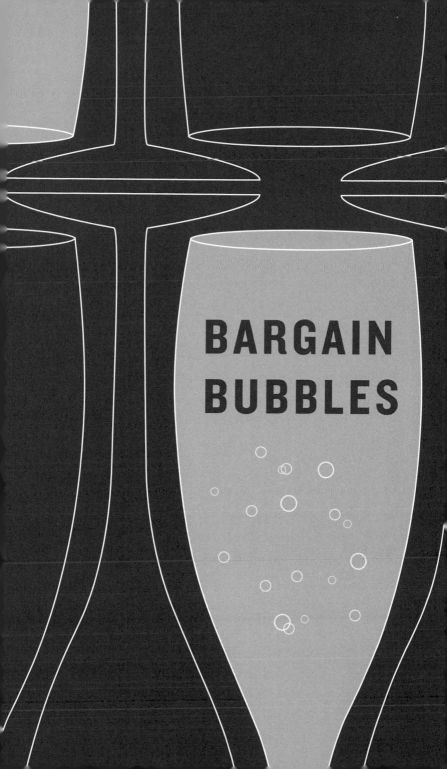

BARGAIN
BUBBLES

ANTECH BLANQUETTE DE LIMOUX

Antech
....
WINERY

Blanquette de Limoux   2007
....
TYPE   YEAR

Limoux, France $20
....
ORIGIN   PRICE   CLOSURE

You've tried champagne. You've tried cava. You've tried Prosecco and Moscato and sparkling wines from Australia, too. Then try this relatively uncommon sparkler. If ever a wine was elegant, it would be this creamy, flowery Blanquette from France's Languedoc region (Limoux is a subregion). Pronounced "ann-TESH," it's made from a grape called Mauzac Blanc ("Blanquette" in Occitan, the region's own language). Lemony, with mild bubbles for those who don't like too much fizz.

TRIVIA Legend has it that a monk named Dom Pérignon invented champagne (and the bubbly wine process), but an abbey (aka monastery) in Limoux has scriptures dating back one hundred years earlier that show how the region's monks made sparkling wine.

PAIR WITH Fresh oysters or sushi. Or drink by itself.

UNCORK At bridal showers, weddings, New Year's Eve parties, dinners with wine geeks or Francophiles. Serve chilled.

ANTECH
— LIMOUX —
2007
BLANQUETTE DE LIMOUX
APPELLATION BLANQUETTE DE LIMOUX CONTRÔLÉE
Réserve Brut
ÉLABORÉ PAR GEORGES ET ROGER ANTECH · 11300 LIMOUX · FRANCE
PRODUIT DE FRANCE

12% vol.   750 ml

ZINCK

Paul Zinck		
WINERY		
Crémant d'Alsace	2007	
TYPE	YEAR	
Alsace, France	$19.50	
ORIGIN	PRICE	CLOSURE

Paul Zinck and his son Philippe are masters when it comes to making a great wine, whatever the varietal, and this Crémant d'Alsace is no exception. From the Alsace region of France, this extremely fragrant white sparkler is made in the traditional champagne method, which is a fancy way of saying it's very good quality.

Oh yeah, and the word *brut* on the label? Just means it's dry.

TRIVIA On the back of the bottle is a little perforated sticker that you can pull off and stick in your wallet so you'll remember the name of the wine and the website. Handy!

PAIR WITH Appetizers such as smoked salmon, sushi, deep-fried calamari, or scallops. Or enjoy by itself.

UNCORK For patio parties, New Year's Eve, weddings, baby showers, birthdays, when you need to impress your Francophile friends. Serve chilled.

UNCORKED

LINI 910

Lini 910
....
WINERY

Lambrusco   non-vintage
....
TYPE   YEAR

Emilia-Romagna, Italy $19
....
ORIGIN   PRICE   CLOSURE

Lambrusco is one of the world's most ancient wines, dating back more than two thousand years. In the 1970s, it was synonymous with a super-sweet, super-cheap sparkler that sold a kazillion bottles.

While sweeter variations are still for sale, today's trendiest Lambrusco—this one—is dry and delicious, with a glorious rose colour. This one leads the pack—and you won't need a disco ball, a tube top, or platform shoes to appreciate it. And it's only available in a couple of places in North America, so you're special just because you live in Alberta. Enjoy!

TRIVIA Lini is made by Alicia Lini, who just happens to be supermodel beautiful as well as a kick-ass winemaker. Her family is celebrating one hundred years of making fantastic Lambrusco in 2010.

PAIR WITH Charcuterie, or serve by itself as an aperitif.

UNCORK Now, at casual Italian-style dinners, patio parties, as a poolside sipper. Serve chilled.

MARCHESI DI BAROLO

Marchesi di Barolo
WINERY

Moscato d'Asti	non-vintage	
TYPE	YEAR	
Italy	$20	
ORIGIN	PRICE	CLOSURE

Moscato is fizzy but it's not the knock-your-socks-off kind of fizz that you'll find in champagne or cava. No, Moscato is floral and delicate, just sweet and flirty enough that you know you're drinking something fun and bubbly. And at only six percent alcohol, you can drink this without getting slammed—at least, without getting slammed quickly.

TRIVIA Apparently, Hollywood star Hilary Swank is a fan of the estate; when she and her brother visited in 2009, they tasted many of the wines, and Swank took home a 1974 Barolo. No word on whether she tried the Moscato d'Asti. I'd pour her a glass.

PAIR WITH Fresh fruit, pound cake, pannacotta.

UNCORK Now, at bridal showers, Mother's Day brunches, or desserts with Italophiles. Serve chilled.

UNCORKED!

PROSECCO DI CONEGLIANO

Canella
....
WINERY

Prosecco   non-vintage
....
TYPE   YEAR

Veneto, Italy $22
....
ORIGIN   PRICE   CLOSURE

This pretty Canella Prosecco gives everyone that insta-party feeling, but without that insta-broke feeling. It smells fruity, but not like shampoo or badly scented candles (like there's any other kind). And it's ever-so-slightly sweet, for those who prefer their only "brut" to be an Ultimate Fighting Champion.

TRIVIA The word *canella* means "cinnamon" in Italian. Prosecco is traditionally added to raspberry and white peach juices to create a Bellini, a tasty (and famous) cocktail that was invented in 1948 in Venice. Make your own with peach purée, raspberry juice, and Prosecco.

PAIR WITH Simple seafood dishes, sushi, fresh raw oysters, salty (and buttery) popcorn. (Yes, I'm serious. I'm always serious.) Or serve as a dinner party aperitif.

UNCORK At brunches, bridal showers, birthday parties, New Year's Eve parties. Serve chilled.

RUSTICO

Nino Franco	Rustico
WINERY	WINE NAME
Prosecco	non-vintage
TYPE	YEAR
Veneto, Italy	$22
ORIGIN	PRICE
	CLOSURE

What's not to love about a winemaker who tells you not to overthink his wines? Just open a bottle and enjoy, he says. So there you have it, folks; we have permission to open this any night of the week because the winemaker, one Primo Franco, says it's meant for fun. That said, this wine will also hold its own when you want to celebrate a special occasion. Or spray it over your head the next time you win a big sporting event.

TRIVIA This dry sparkler comes from Valdobbiadene. Say that ten times fast. (FYI, it's in Italy's Veneto region, near Venice.) Prosecco is both the style of wine and the name of the grape.

PAIR WITH Sushi, risotto, hard cheese, salty almonds, popcorn, or potato chips, or drink as an aperitif.

UNCORK Now, for New Year's Eve, weddings, birthdays. Serve chilled.

VILLA TERESA

Villa Teresa
....
WINERY

Prosecco   non-vintage
....
TYPE   YEAR

Veneto, Italy $15
....
ORIGIN   PRICE   CLOSURE

BARGAIN BUBBLES

What's not to love about a bottle of wine that's packaged more like, well, beer? This old school flip-top closure can be resealed if you don't finish your bottle all in one go. Or wash it out when you're done and reuse it to store homemade salad dressings. Prosecco is incredibly food-friendly, and versatile, too. And as a bonus, it's organic.

TRIVIA Located close to Venice, the winery was started in 1936 and is still owned by the same family.

PAIR WITH Salad, roasted almonds, popcorn, prosciutto, calamari, Chinese food.

UNCORK At picnics, New Year's Eve parties, weddings, Earth Day celebrations. Serve chilled.

PARÉS BALTÀ

Parés Baltà
WINERY

cava	non-vintage	
TYPE	YEAR	
Spain	$19	
ORIGIN	PRICE	CLOSURE

Parés Baltà is the kind of winery that reminds you that vineyards are about farming. A herd of sheep wander through the vineyards, providing natural fertilization. (I'll spare you the graphic details here.) And beehives help in pollination. Real farming, real life, real organics in action. And the folks at Parés Baltà aren't just about avoiding chemicals; they're about water conservation, too. None of the vines are irrigated, meaning any water they get comes from the rain. This process stresses the vines, creating what many believe to be better grapes.

You'll believe it, too, once you try this creamy, toasty honey of a bubbly, made in the traditional champagne method.

TRIVIA Female winemakers are rare—not just in Spain but everywhere. This winery is owned by the founder's two grandsons, and their wives, Maria Elena Jimenez and Marta Casas, are the winemakers.

PAIR WITH Oysters, shrimp, scallops, hard Spanish-style cheeses, fresh in-season fruit, potato chips, popcorn. Or drink by itself.

UNCORK For bullfights, dinner with wine geeks, New Year's Eve, weddings, baby showers, birthdays. Serve chilled.

UNCORKED

SEGURA VIUDAS

Segura Viudas
WINERY

cava	non-vintage	
TYPE	YEAR	

Penedès, Spain	$17	
ORIGIN	PRICE	CLOSURE

Champagne is generally pretty pricey, but this cava is made following the traditional champagne method—and it costs a whole lot less. The word *cava* is simply an official Spanish word for sparkling wine made in Spain—and only in Spain. This very dry ("brut" on the label means it's dry) sparkler is all apples and lime and cream soda; it's a blend of three traditional Spanish cava grapes, Macabeo, Parellada, and Xarel-lo (yes, the odd little dash is intentional there).

TRIVIA Segura Viudas was founded in 1950, the same year the Korean War started, Bob Hope's television specials began broadcasting, and Disney released *Cinderella*. Find the winery on Facebook by searching for Segura Viudas.

PAIR WITH Fresh oysters, crab cakes, popcorn, sushi.

UNCORK Now, on New Year's Eve, for weddings, baby showers, birthdays, when your favourite team wins. Serve chilled.

SEAVIEW

Seaview
....
WINERY

sparkling white blend	non-vintage
TYPE	YEAR

South Eastern Australia	$14	
ORIGIN	PRICE	CLOSURE

Sometimes you just need a super affordable sparkling wine that you can share with friends, that you can turn into mimosas or Bellinis or cocktails, or just drink and enjoy. This is that wine. Fresh and a little bit fruity, it's one you can open any time you need a wee bit of bubbly but don't want to feel guilty if you don't get around to finishing the bottle.

TRIVIA To make a mimosa, pour half a glass of sparkling wine. Top it off with orange juice and garnish with a slice of strawberry. Voilà—a brunch cocktail.

PAIR WITH Appetizers such as smoked salmon or sushi. Or turn into Bellinis, mimosas, or other bubbly cocktails.

UNCORK At brunches, New Year's Eve parties, patio parties. Serve chilled.

UNCORKED

NIETO SENETINER

Nieto Senetiner
....
WINERY

sparkling blend   non-vintage
....
TYPE   YEAR

Mendoza, Argentina $24
....
ORIGIN   PRICE   CLOSURE

Ever go to one of those New Year's parties where someone opens a bottle of $100-plus champagne just before midnight, but everyone's so drunk by this point that they 1) don't notice or care, or 2) barely try a sip and then leave their almost-full glasses sitting around the house? Heartbreaking. In those situations, it's all I can do to keep from running around the room, downing everyone's leftovers. That's the time when you need to whip out something like this sparkler from South America. It's an affordable little taste of luxury.

TRIVIA The winery gets its name from Nicanor Nieto and Adriano Senetiner, who bought the place in 1969; it's now owned by the family of Gregorio Pérez Companc, Argentina's richest person, if you believe what you read on the Internet.

PAIR WITH Fresh oysters, sushi, popcorn, potato chips. Or serve as an aperitif.

UNCORK Now, for New Year's Eve, weddings, birthdays. Serve chilled.

SWEET &
FORTIFIED
WINES

FIELD STONE FRUIT WINES

Field Stone Fruit Wines

WINERY

Saskatoon berry dessert wine	non-vintage	
TYPE	YEAR	

Strathmore, Alberta	$20 for 375 mL	
ORIGIN	PRICE	CLOSURE

Alberta has wineries. Not just one—a few (fruit wineries, that is). This one, Field Stone, was started in 2005 and is located about half an hour east of Calgary; stop in for a tour if you're around on a summer weekend. The family-owned operation makes several dessert wines and table wines, mostly from locally grown fruit. If saskatoons aren't your favourite, consider some of their other offerings: black currant, strawberry-rhubarb, wild black cherry, and more. Add a sparkling wine to a bit of the saskatoon for a locavore kir royale—a Canuck take on the classic French cocktail—if you're looking for something fancy.

TRIVIA Saskatoons are tough little berries that look a bit like blueberries but have their own distinctive taste. Unlike blueberries, they thrive in Alberta, despite our unpredictable winters.

PAIR WITH Homemade vanilla ice cream, plain cheesecake, angel food cake, and whipped cream, or serve solo.

UNCORK For locavore dinners, 100-mile diets, bridal showers, weddings, Sunday evening desserts in winter, any time you need a pretty dessert wine and you're feeling too cheap to buy icewine. Serve chilled.

ESSENSIA

Quady Winery	Essensia	
WINERY	WINE NAME	
dessert wine	2007	
TYPE	YEAR	
California	$15 for 375 mL	
ORIGIN	PRICE	CLOSURE

This wine is pretty (a lovely orange colour) and smells good (aromas of orange blossoms, honey, apricot, vanilla) and tastes good (notes of tangerines and honey). Sweet but not too, too sweet.

Andrew and Laurel Quady—the couple who started the winery—recommend trying a shot of Essensia with sparkling wine, to make an "Essensia Royale." Try a few of those with scones and fresh seasonal fruit at your next brunch. No one will remember that you scorched the coffee.

TRIVIA Andrew Quady worked in pyrotechnics (yeah, fireworks) and munitions before starting up Quady Winery in the 1970s.

PAIR WITH Plain pound cake and whipped cream, or alongside a plain flan. Or serve little glasses of it solo.

UNCORK For brunches, Granny's birthday, bridal showers, birthday parties, when the boss is coming to dinner, when you're cooking for the in-laws for the first time, when you're cooking for the in-laws for the umpteenth time. Serve chilled.

UNCORKED!

CHÂTEAU LOUPIAC-GAUDIET

Château Loupiac-Gaudiet

WINERY

dessert wine	2003
TYPE	YEAR

Loupiac, France	$16 for 375 mL	
ORIGIN	PRICE	CLOSURE

Don't be alarmed when you see that this bottle is small, exactly half the size of a regular table wine. That's the way it's supposed to be. This delicious, rich, aromatic sweet wine is from France's Loupiac region, a sweet-wine region in Bordeaux that is literally just across the river from one of the world's most famous sweet wines, Sauternes. Think of the wine as the poor man's (or poor woman's) Château d'Yquem. It's made from 80 percent Sémillon and 20 percent Sauvignon Blanc, and the vines are at least thirty-five years old.

TRIVIA Wines in this region are made sweet with the help of a fungus (*Botrytis cinerea*) that generally goes by the rather poetic name of "noble rot." The fungus turns grapes into shrivelled raisinish bits that are filled with sweet, concentrated juice.

PAIR WITH Foie gras, cheese, fresh fruit.

UNCORK For birthdays (well, if you're eighteen or older), turkey day (for dessert), dinners with Francophiles, impressing the wine geeks.

DOMAINE FORÇA RÉAL

Domaine Força Réal	Rivesaltes Hors d'Age	
WINERY	WINE NAME	
dessert wine	non-vintage	
TYPE	YEAR	
Languedoc-Roussillon, France	$19 for 500 mL	
ORIGIN	PRICE	CLOSURE

Maybe you think a sweet wine will taste like cough medicine, the syrupy stuff that made you wish like hell you could stop hacking so your mom wouldn't make you swallow it.

Don't worry. This Rivesaltes is not that taste. Oh no. I will warn you, however, that you may not want to share this one with anyone else. Well, maybe with someone you really, really love. Really, really lots. One chilly sip and you will want to run away to the South of France, where you will find more, more, more. A rich, dark amber colour, the wine tastes (and smells) of marmalade and toasted nuts.

TRIVIA The term *hors d'age* on a label, any label, means the wine (or other booze) inside has been well aged, usually for at least ten years.

PAIR WITH Foie gras, cheese, almond desserts, or, as the label suggests, with anchovies on toast. Um, yeah. Or drink by itself.

UNCORK Now, for New Year's Eve, birthday parties (the significant ones), anniversaries, dinners with Francophiles, turkey-day desserts. Or stick in the cellar for a few years. Serve chilled.

LUSTAU

Lustau	East India Solera	
WINERY	WINE NAME	
sherry	non-vintage	
TYPE	YEAR	
Jerez, Spain	$18 for 375 mL	
ORIGIN	PRICE	CLOSURE

Sherry is one of the world's oldest and greatest wines, and while it's not to everyone's taste, every wine lover should try it at least once. And if legwarmers and Teenage Mutant Ninja Turtles can come back in style, then sherry should have its day in the sun again one day, too. Here's to being at the vanguard of a new trend.

This sherry is sweeter than most, and smells like raisins, nuts, and Christmas fruitcake. Unlike fruitcake, you don't want to give it away as soon as someone gives it to you. But watch out: the alcohol content is 20 percent, about 8 percent more than most wines.

TRIVIA The solera process was invented to even out quality between vintage years (you'll notice this bottle doesn't have a specific year on it). Every year, a little wine is removed (and bottled) from the oldest barrels and replaced with wine from the next-oldest barrels, and so on.

PAIR WITH Dark chocolate, cheese, Christmas pudding. Or serve solo at the end of a meal.

UNCORK For turkey day, impressing a wine geek, the first snowfall of the season.

FONSECA

Fonseca	Bin No. 27 Reserve
WINERY	WINE NAME
port	non-vintage
TYPE	YEAR
Douro Valley, Portugal	$22
ORIGIN	PRICE

CLOSURE

Do you like big, jammy, full-bodied red wines? Then try port. Port wines are fortified, meaning that hard alcohol (spirits) is added to the wine to stop the fermentation process, the process that normally turns all that juice into what we know as wine. A fortified wine can't have the word *port* on the label unless it comes from Portugal's Douro Valley, home to the real deal. This port is pretty much what it sounds like, a sweet beauty of a wine that's ready to drink now. A great introduction to the world of port and fortified wines.

TRIVIA Bin 27 was the vat closest to the house of the late Fonseca port winemaker Bruce Guimaraens; when he went to fetch a decanter of "house port," it was from Bin 27. The family's house port wasn't released commercially until 1972.

PAIR WITH Nuts, cheeses (especially blue cheese). Or drink by itself.

UNCORK Now, for the first snowfall of the year, January cold spells, spring snowfalls. Chill slightly (a little cooler than room temperature).

UNCORKED!

PFEIFFER

Pfeiffer
....
WINERY

Muscat   non-vintage
....
TYPE   YEAR

Rutherglen, Australia $18 for 500 mL
....
ORIGIN   PRICE   CLOSURE

Muscat is the grape that's been used to make this fortified dessert wine, which, although it technically doesn't have a vintage, is blended from wines that are at least ten years old.

TRIVIA The winery was started by Chris Pfeiffer, but the winemaker here is his daughter, Jen Pfeiffer. She worked briefly for the Taylor Fladgate port producers, which, according to the Pfeiffer website, "is sure to help her achieve her goal of becoming Australia's Princess of Port."

PAIR WITH Chocolate cake, vanilla ice cream, Christmas pudding, poached fruit, cheese, flan, pannacotta. Or enjoy by itself.

UNCORK Now, for turkey-day dessert, dinner with the boss, meeting his/her parents for the first time, the first snow-fall of the year. Serve chilled.

ERRAZURIZ

Viña Errázuriz
WINERY

late harvest Sauvignon Blanc	2008	
TYPE	YEAR	

Casablanca, Chile	$15	
ORIGIN	PRICE	CLOSURE

This cheerful sweetie costs considerably less than icewine yet gives a similar sweet kick at the end of a meal. It's a sweetness that's not cloying; you won't feel like you're drinking cough medicine if you take a swig. Honest.

As for the winery, it's been owned by the same family for more than 130 years; president Eduardo Chadwick is a direct descendent of Don Maximiano Errázuriz, who started the winery in the Aconcagua Valley; the family now owns property in many of Chile's top wine-producing regions.

TRIVIA Don Maximiano Errázuriz, the winery's founder, was a famous (and wealthy) Chilean politician who owned a copper mining company. At one point, he backed up his government by lending it money. His own money.

PAIR WITH Plain pound cake, angel food cake, flan topped with fresh mango or berries. Or serve by itself in tiny glasses.

UNCORK Now, or as a cel-ebratory drink at the end of fancy dinner parties. Serve chilled.

SHELLEY'S DESERT ISLAND WINES

Choosing only a handful of my favourite wines in this book is hard, almost impossible. But if I could only take a dozen wines with me to a desert island, here are the ones I'd choose:

REDS
Blue Mountain Vineyard and Cellars Gamay Noir 2009 (page 6)
Gray Monk Estate Winery 'Latitude 50' 2008 (page 9)
No. 99 Wayne Gretzky Estates Cabernet-Merlot 2007 (page 13)
Fattoria Poggerino 'Il Labirinto' Chianti 2007 (page 40)
Tsantali Organic Cabernet Sauvignon 2006 (page 65)

WHITES
Cave Spring Beamsville Bench Estate Bottled Riesling 2007 (page 101)
Château de Jau 'Le Jaja de Jau' Sauvignon Blanc 2008 (page 111)
Lingenfelder 'Bird Label' Riesling 2007 (page 115)

ROSÉ
Château Ollieux Romanis Rosé 2008 (page 136)

BUBBLES
Paul Zinck Brut Crémant d'Alsace 2007 (page 143)
Parés Baltà Brut Cava (page 149)

SWEET
Quady Winery 'Essensia' Dessert Wine 2007 (page 155)

WHERE TO BUY THESE WINES

Many of these wines are available at wine shops across the province. If you're looking for a particular label, however, and you can't find it, try the following:

GO TO ALBERTA-LIQUOR-GUIDE.COM.

This site is run by the Alberta government, and you can search to find the name of the importer and, in most cases, individual stores that carry or have carried the product. Call to ensure stock before you show up and demand a case.

CHECK OUT SOME OF THE ONLINE SHOPPING SITES.

At least two, Zyn.ca (403-543-8900) and WineOnline.ca (or call 1-877-714-WINE), can ship wines across the province. The Wine Cavern in Lethbridge can ship across the province, but you can't order wines online; you'll have to call to order (see TheWineCavern.com or call 403-320-1133). Or try Willow Park Wines & Spirits (WillowPark.net or 1-403-296-1640); they can ship across the province. Others, such as KensingtonWineMarket.com (1-888-283-9004), can ship within Calgary.

FURTHER RESOURCES

READ A BOOK

Want to read more about wine? There are dozens of great books out there that will inspire you and further your wine knowledge. Here are a few of my favourites:

Champagne for Dummies by Ed McCarthy (John Wiley & Sons)

Discovering Wine: A Refreshingly Unfussy Beginner's Guide to Finding, Tasting, Judging, Storing, Serving, Cellaring, and, Most of All, Discovering Wine by Joanna Simon (Simon & Schuster)

Eating & Drinking: An A–Z of Great Food and Drink Combinations by Fiona Beckett (Mitchell Beazley, out of print, but if you can track down a used copy, buy it!)

Kevin Zraly's Windows on the World Complete Wine Course: 25th Anniversary Edition (Sterling Publishing)

The Oxford Companion to Wine, edited by Jancis Robinson (Oxford University Press)

Tony Aspler's Cellar Book: How to Design, Build, Stock and Manage Your Wine Cellar Wherever You Live (Random House Canada)

Wine: An Introduction by Joanna Simon (Dorling Kindersley)

WineWise: Your Complete Guide to Understanding, Selecting and Enjoying Wine by Steven Kolpan, Brian H. Smith, and Michael A. Weiss, The Culinary Institute of North America (John Wiley & Sons)

The World Atlas of Wine by Hugh Johnson and Jancis Robinson (Mitchell Beazley)

TAKE A CLASS

Many large wine stores offer tastings and seminars, or ask the sommeliers at your favourite local restaurants if they host winemakers' dinners.

Or check out the following:

- The Wine & Spirit Education Trust (WSET, wset.co.uk) offers courses around the world, including in Calgary, and if you pass the exam at the end, you'll achieve international certification—handy, in case you ever need to impress, oh, say for example, a cute single person at a wine bar on the other side of the globe.
- The International Sommelier Guild (www.internationalsommelier .com) is another internationally recognized certificate program. Like the WSET program, there are different levels. Take just one, or work your way to the top.
- The European Wine Academy (europeanwineacademy.org) offers courses in English for beginners, professionals, and wannabe professionals. Some of the courses are offered online, so it doesn't matter where you live.

ACKNOWLEDGEMENTS

Thank you—
To Anders, Erik, and Steen for putting up with me. To my parents, who started me on my wine journey. To my family (especially Doug, Shirley, Mike, and Annette) and my friends, who are always willing to taste wine with me. To all of my friends in the wine industry in Canada and beyond who supplied bottles, advice, labels, and more. To my friends at the *Calgary Herald* and *Wine Access*. And to Robert, Michelle, Setareh, Jesse, Taryn, Sarah, Cameron, and Grace—the creative bunch at Whitecap. Without your hard work, this book would still be just an idea in my head.

INDEX

Looking for new ways to taste wine at home? Consider buying a few bottles (same grape, different regions) to taste and compare. Throw a Cabernet Cabaret, or Mingle amongst the Merlots!

Grapes make up most of the main headings in this index; you'll also find categories like *Prosecco* and *port*, and a number of Old World appellations and regions in Canada and the U.S. Flip to the table of contents at the front of the book if you want to go to the wines of a specific country.

UNCORKED!

ABOUT THE AUTHOR

Born and raised in Alberta, Shelley Boettcher is the executive editor at *Wine Access* magazine, and a weekly wine columnist and blogger at the *Calgary Herald*. Her stories have appeared in magazines and newspapers around the world. She holds a master's degree in journalism from the University of Western Ontario, and an intermediate wine and spirits certificate from the Wine and Spirit Education Trust. She has also studied with the International Sommelier Guild. Boettcher has been a judge at Vinitaly, one of the world's largest wine fairs, and she has interviewed many renowned winemakers, including Wolf Blass and Penfolds's Peter Gago. Her favourite wine? Whatever she's drinking at the moment. She can be reached through her website at shelleyboettcher.com or follow her on Twitter at @shelley_wine. Ten percent of the author's proceeds from the sale of this book go to Grapes for Humanity (grapesforhumanity.com).

photo: Anders Knudsen